A Disturbing Thing Happened Today

By

Conrad Jones

A Disturbing Thing Happened Today
Copyright 2022 © Conrad Jones
All Rights Reserved.

No part of this publication may be reproduced, distributed, or transmitted in any form or by any means, or stored in a database or retrieval system, without prior documented approval of the publisher.

This book is a work of fiction.

Names, characters, places, and incidents either are the products of the author's imagination or are used fictitiously.

Any resemblance to actual persons, living or dead, businesses, companies, events, or locales is entirely coincidental.

A Disturbing Thing Happened Today...

Chapter 1

Detective Chief Inspector Alan Williams checked his watch again. His DI, Kim Davies was over an hour late, which was unheard of. It was completely out of character, and it was making him feel unsettled. Something was wrong; he sensed it. Her father had been an overbearing bully with a hatred of tardiness, which led to her having a phobia of being late for anything. He used to tell her she would be late for her own funeral, which was a disturbing thought for a little girl. She was actually late for his funeral by three days, but that was intentional. His influence meant Kim arrived early to meetings, functions, interviews, and every single shift to avoid the issue raising its head. Other people being late drove her to distraction, which amused Alan no end. Alan had been managing police officers for decades and he realised employees are occasionally late, but not Kim. Never. Something was amiss.

Alan felt uneasy but couldn't put his finger on the reason why. It was a gut feeling. He had trusted his gut feeling many times through his career, and his first instinct was usually the right one. His knee ached, and he rubbed at the pain but there was something more than arthritis seeping through his bones. He felt a sense of dread creeping deep inside him, concentrated in the pit of his stomach and spreading like a cancer through his bones.

A knock on his door disturbed his thoughts, and he looked up to see DS Richard Lewis pop his head around the door. His grey hair was wispy and wild and his ruddy cheeks told Alan he had only just arrived in the building.

'Alanio,' he said, cheerily. 'Good morning to you. I trust all is as well as it should be?'

'You look windswept and cold,' Alan said. The island's winds had played havoc with his head on the short walk from his car into the station. 'My recycling trolley was last seen heading across the fields towards Rhoscolyn.'

'Another one gone,' Richard said, shaking his head as if they'd lost a valued friend. 'That's what comes of living on a rock in the Irish Sea,' Richard said, trying to smooth his hair down. The Anglesey winds paid no attention to hairstyles, no matter how well sprayed or gelled. He looked like a mad professor on a bad day. 'It's a cross we must bear to dwell in God's country.'

'It is indeed,' Alan said.

'I'm making a drink,' Richard said. 'Do you want a brew?'

'Yes, please,' Alan replied. 'Have you heard from Kim this morning?'

'Not yet,' Richard said, checking the clock. 'She's late.'

'She is,' Alan said, smiling thinly. 'Considering this building is full of detectives, I'm glad it's not just me who noticed she isn't here.'

'She's never late for anything,' Richard said.

'Exactly. That's why I asked if you'd heard from her.'

'She's not on holiday, is she?'

'I don't think so,' Alan said, frowning. He looked embarrassed. His admin skills were notoriously crap. He began to search on his laptop. 'She might be. I'll have a look.'

'It wouldn't be the first time you've forgotten when one of us is on a holiday.' Richard looked thoughtful. He scratched his chin. 'In fact, you do it all the time.'

'I think that's an exaggeration.'

'Not really,' Richard disagreed.

'I'm aware of the odd oversight, thank you for pointing it out,' Alan muttered. He pulled up the holiday schedule on his laptop. 'Nope. She's not on holiday.'

'Which means she's late and she's never late,' Richard pointed out. 'Do you want me to call her?'

'Best if I do it. I'll call her mobile,' Alan said. 'If you ring her, she'll know I've told you to and I don't want her to think I'm checking up on her.'

'She'll think you're checking up on her whatever you do. You can't win,' Richard said, shaking his head. He frowned. 'Don't delay though,' he warned. 'She lives alone and could have fallen down the stairs and broken her neck. She might be lying in a heap in the hallway at the bottom of the stairs unable to move.'

'Thanks for that image, Richard,' Alan said.

'Or she may be having a heart attack. She's in the right age bracket.'

'Shut up.'

'Delaying making the call could be fatal and if she dies, she'll blame you from the afterlife. Then she'll haunt you forever,' he added. 'That would be a nightmare.'

'I can't risk that,' Alan said. 'I don't want her face popping up in the mirror every time I go for a shave, scaring the shit out of me.'

'Or making your bed shake,' Richard said. 'There's always a bit of bed shaking in every good haunting.' He nodded and his jowls wobbled. 'Best to be on the safe side. Anyway, I'll make the brews while you make contact.' Richard closed the door.

Alan dialled Kim and waited. The phone rang twelve times and switched to voicemail. He cut off the call without leaving a message and scrolled to her home number. The line was dead. He checked his watch again and walked to the window. Holyhead Police Station was situated in the centre of town, a stone's throw from the tiny cinema. His office looked over the old library and the car park. Her car wasn't there. There was a car park at the back of the station but it was tight and full by nine o'clock. If she'd arrived recently, she would have to park at the front. His head was full of questions like why was her landline dead?

Alan couldn't shrug the overwhelming feeling of foreboding. He felt something was about to happen. Something enormous. Something bad. Every nerve ending in his body was tingling. He decided to go to her home and check on her. She might be sick but that didn't explain why she wasn't answering her mobile. He grabbed his wax jacket from the back of his chair. Kim lived on the Gorad Road in Valley. It was a ten-minute drive. He opened his office door and rushed out, crashing into Richard, who was carrying a tray of drinks. Tea and coffee sprayed everyone in close vicinity and the cups clattered onto the floor and smashed. A round of applause broke out across the office.

'Sack the juggler!'

'Oops. Butter fingers.'

'Oh, for fuck's sake,' Alan said, wiping coffee from his shirt and tie. 'These were clean on this week,' he muttered. 'Sorry. That was my fault,' he said. Richard was red-faced.

'I know whose fault it was,' Richard said, nodding. 'Yours. Rushing about like a bull in a China shop.' He frowned when he noticed Alan had his jacket in his hand. 'I gather you haven't got hold of her?'

'No.' Alan shook his head and dabbed at his shirt with a piece of kitchen roll. 'She's not picking up and her landline is dead.'

'Not connecting at all?' Richard asked.

'No. It's completely dead.'

'That's not good,' Richard said.

'I know it isn't,' Alan muttered, irritated.

'I'll drive,' Richard said. 'This has obviously disturbed you.'

'I'm fine.'

'No. You're obviously not able to coordinate yourself around the office, let alone drive.'

'I'll drive,' Alan said, shaking his head. 'I want to get there today.'

'Charming,' Richard said. 'I'll get my coat.'

'Do you want any back-up?' DS Chris Hall asked from a nearby desk. He was known as Chod. 'Better to be safe than sorry.'

'Thanks, Chod,' Alan said. 'It can't hurt. We'll see you there.'

Chapter 2

Ernie Metcalfe watched dozens of kids walking to the school at Menai Bridge. They ambled up the hill in groups, some in pairs, and some solo. A myriad of youths of every shape and size and all the colours of the rainbow headed through the gates. As he watched them, he remembered being that age. They were all full of both hope and anxiety for what their lives would become. Accountants, artists, musicians, bricklayers, farmers, fashion designers, hairdressers, politicians, layabouts, rapists, and murderers. Some would succeed and some would fail. A few would die young before they had the chance to reach their potential, while others would live long lives, forever disappointed at what life brought them. At that age, he remembered life was a lottery that not everyone could win. Age and experience brought with them the knowledge that each day was a gamble, an adventure, and a gift for some and a constant struggle for others.

He studied each one as they passed by. Some of them laughed and clowned around. Others looked morose and miserable. A few looked excited to be there while others looked like they were taking the long walk to the gallows. He had been watching on and off for over a week now. Today was the day to stop watching and act. Protecting his daughters was his single focus now his wife Naomi was dead. She had died in a car crash three years earlier. A car crash he had manufactured and survived. God had taken her because she had been an unfaithful slut and Ernie was glad, she was dead although he had to admit he missed her, in fact, he missed her terribly. Naomi had been the love of his life and his one true love and he genuinely believed there could be no other. She had betrayed him in the worst possible way and cheated on him. She had broken his heart but it was all in the past now. The difference between the quick and the dead was life itself and she had gambled hers and lost. He was still breathing while she was rotting in the ground and that felt like universal justice.

Since her death, his daughters had become his focus and Helen, his eldest, was in danger. She was an attractive girl and had become the focus of a fifteen-year-old boy called Rio Woods and that focus needed to be deflected. Ernie was aware she'd already appeared on a number of sexual radars as she headed into adolescence, but they had fizzled out and come to nothing. This threat was persistent, and he needed to intervene. Rio Woods had latched onto her, sending her messages over a period of weeks and his messages had become unacceptably suggestive. He was grooming his thirteen-year-old daughter and that was unacceptable.

Ernie had installed a Trojan Horse into her mobile. Every text message she received was also sent to his phone. When her phone rang, his rang too and he could hear her conversations. It was intrusive but she would never know the spyware was installed unless he told her. He was her father and he had to know what she was up to and who with so that he could protect her from male interest. Slut.

Her body was changing but she was thirteen and still a vulnerable child, despite her protestations. Hormones and pheromones were beginning to flow in her and in the kids she associated with. School was awash with testosterone as the teenagers became sexually aware. Some of her friends were already Instagram queens, posing and pouting like models and they looked much older than their years. It was filter this and filter that and it was fucking dangerous. Their flirtatiousness at such a young age made his stomach churn. Sluts.

He had seen a few messages from boys and they were innocent enough but this new boy Rio Woods was a few years above her in school and he was a problem. He was pushing the boundaries and becoming more intense to the point where he had crossed the line and needed to be eliminated from her life. Permanently if necessary. Ernie had messaged the teenager directly and told him to cease and desist but the cocky little bastard had told him to 'take a chill-pill'. Apparently, there was nothing to worry about; they were just friends. Ernie had approached the subject with Helen but she had blushed and stormed off to her room, where she had spent the night crying and playing ballads over and over. His mother, Rose, who had lived with them since his father had died the year before, had told him to go lightly on the subject. Teenagers were full of hormones and the worst thing he could do was dictate to her who she could be friends with and who she couldn't. Rose said she had to learn to deal with approaches from the opposite sex herself. They were a fact of life that she would have to deal with not only as a young woman but all the way through her life. She said men were permanently like dogs on heat sniffing at the backsides of females and it was to be expected that she'd receive attention from them as she matured. Dealing with sexual advances would become a life skill for her and she needed to master it.

Ernie said that was bullshit. She was thirteen for God's sake and she was her mother's daughter and her mother had been a slut. Naomi was taking it up the arse from his colleague until he found out and when he found out, she died. Maybe the apple hadn't fallen far from the tree. Ernie was well aware of what was going on. The males of the species spent most of their lives trying to fuck the females or other males depending on their preference. Some did both, apparently. Males were genetically programmed to procreate, and their sexual instincts were powerful and difficult to control. They had to fuck something on a regular basis, even if it was themselves. The pornography industry had become an untameable monster unleashed on humanity via the internet. Teenagers had more access to porn in their pocket than his generation could have imagined in their wildest nightmares. Their obsession with sex was unrivalled by previous generations and unhealthy. He understood better than most the disasters that could be caused by sexual desire but that's what parents were for. They were there to nurture and protect their children from the dangers that life presented. Rio Woods was a danger and a persistent one at that. Ernie wasn't going to allow his child to be the focus of an adolescent wet dream. He'd tried the polite route to deter Rio and it hadn't worked. It was time to deploy a more powerful method. Fear.

Ernie waited for Rio and his friends to appear on the far side of the Dingle car park. They used a path which followed the stream through a copse. He was with the usual group of friends he walked to school with. There was no urgency to get there; they ambled along oblivious of the time. They were going to be late for school but they were late every day. It clearly wasn't an issue for them. The others in the group were throwing stones at a boy on the opposite side of the stream. Rio was at the back of the group, glued to his phone and smoking a cigarette. His friends began to chase the boy who was fifty yards ahead of them. The boy turned and flicked them the finger before sprinting for the safety of the playground, which was being monitored by a burly teacher with a clipboard and huge beard. He wore a whistle around his neck, which screamed PE teacher.

The pursuit meant the group were way ahead of their friend. It was the perfect opportunity. Rio was alone and vulnerable. Vulnerable like his thirteen-year-old daughter. It was time to spell things out to the boy, so that he was under no illusions what would happen if he didn't stop pestering Helen. Ernie opened the door and climbed out. He jogged silently across the car park to a clump of trees where he waited unseen next to the path.

Ironically, Rio was sending his daughter a suggestive message on TikTok and was unaware of the danger lurking ahead of him as he approached.

CHAPTER 3

Alan parked outside Kim's house and turned off the engine, while making a quick study of the windows. All the curtains were closed except the bedroom. She never closed the curtains until bedtime, they made her feel claustrophobic. One of the bedroom curtains was half open and hanging at an awkward angle. The material was twisted the wrong way, showing the lining. Some of the hooks were visible, as if it had been ripped from its fastening. Alan felt his anxiety rising.

'Where does she park her car?' Richard asked.

'She puts it in the garage,' Alan said. 'Every night without fail. She's a creature of habit and she opens all the curtains as soon as she wakes up on the way to switching on the kettle.'

'The bedroom curtain has been pulled down.'

'I can see that,' Alan said.

'That doesn't look good,' Richard said, climbing out. 'If we can't get in, who has a spare key?'

'I do,' Alan said, reaching for it as he climbed out too. They'd been in a relationship of sorts for as long as he could remember, but it wasn't discussed with colleagues. Everyone at the station knew they had a thing, but nobody mentioned it. They'd tried to have a traditional relationship but living together hadn't worked for either of them. They were both too set in their ways.

Alan left the BMW open and jogged towards the front door. His hand was shaking a little when he slid the key into the lock. Richard pressed the doorbell just in case. 'What are you doing that for?' Alan asked.

'I'm just being polite,' Richard said. He shrugged. 'She might be in the bath.'

'She isn't in the bath,' Alan muttered.

Alan pushed the door open and absorbed the atmosphere. There was a faint odour of bleach. He stepped into the hallway his senses ultra-aware. There was a sickly-sweet smell of sweat in the air. It was alien to the house and didn't belong to Kim. It was a male scent. He sensed that immediately. The living room to the left was pristine, everything in its place except for a single wine glass on the coffee table. There was an inch of white wine in the bottom. She drank three glasses of chardonnay every night. Sometimes she drank more, but rarely less. It helped her sleep, but she never left any and the glass was put into the sink on her way to bed. It was her routine, and she never deviated from it.

'Check the kitchen. I'll look upstairs,' Alan said. Richard walked down the hallway. Alan climbed the stairs, his footsteps hardly audible. The carpet was grey, appearing almost silver in daylight, and he noticed darker patches on some of the treads. He touched one of the patches. It was wet. He smelt his fingers and got a whiff of bleach and something else. Maybe washing detergent.

He reached the landing and saw a large stain. The smell of bleach was stronger now. Someone had cleaned something from the carpet in the last few hours. Alan wanted to call her name, but knew it was pointless. He pushed open the bathroom door and the odour of excrement hit him. The toilet had been flushed, but the stench lingered and there was heavy staining above the waterline. Kim would have died before she left her toilet in that condition. It was another sign that at least one other had been in the house recently. His heart was beating faster with each step he took towards the bedroom. The images of a hundred crime scenes flashed through his mind. Faces of the dead paraded in his mind, raped, murdered, rotten, and decomposed. He stopped at the door for a millisecond before pushing it open slowly.

Alan felt a slight movement behind the door. There was a minute shift in the weight and speed at which it opened. His fingertips were on the handle as it opened as if in slow motion. He saw the image of Kim in his mind. She was sitting on the bed, her arms outstretched like a crucifix and bound at the wrists to the wrought iron headboard. Blood streaked her nose and lips, congealing on her skin. Her eyes were wide and frightened. Mascara streaked her cheeks. She shook her head wildly, warning him, begging him not to enter. He blinked, and the image was gone. Her bed was empty, and the bedding had been removed, but the warning lingered in his brain.

In a millisecond, he noticed a glint of light reflecting from a gossamer-like thread, which was attached to the door handle. It was like fishing twine, transparent and strong. He followed the twine with his eyes to see what it was attached to. His confusion was only momentary. The roar of a shotgun deafened him. Both barrels fired, and the blast hit him like an express train. He felt the lead shot piercing his skin in a dozen places simultaneously. The impact knocked him off his feet. White hot pain radiated from every inch of his being. Muscle was ripped and torn, and bone was cracked and broken. His brain couldn't cope with the catastrophic damage. It only registered for a nanosecond before he was engulfed in scorching darkness as he hit the floor.

CHAPTER 4

Ernie listened to the approaching footsteps and waited until Rio drew level with him. The boy saw movement from the corner of his eye and he half turned, surprised and frightened for a moment. He was startled and uneasy.

'What the fuck, man?' Rio stammered.

'You're Rio Woods,' Ernie said, stepping out to block his path. The boy nodded, fear and recognition in his eyes. 'I'm Ernest Metcalfe. I'm Helen's father.'

'I thought I recognised you. I know who you are,' Rio said, nodding. He took a drag of his cigarette to calm his nerves.

'We've never met,' Ernie said.

'I recognise you from Helen's Facebook.'

'Ah. I see,' Ernie said, nodding.

'There are photos from a barbeque you had for Hannah's birthday last month. She showed me them.'

'Who showed you them?' Ernie asked.

'Helen.'

'When?'

'I don't know for sure,' Rio said. 'A few weeks ago. We were chatting, and she told me about the barbeque.'

'Did she really?' Ernie said, shaking his head with frustration. 'Family events should be kept private, especially the photographs. They're not for every man and his dog to paw over. Facebook has a lot to answer for.'

'Social media is king, mate. It's here to stay,' Rio said, shrugging. 'It's nothing to lose your shit over. They're just photographs of your barbeque. No big deal.'

'It's a big deal to me. Much bigger than you realise, so I must disagree with you.'

'Whatever, mate. They're just photographs.'

'Your interest in my daughters and their photographs is why I'm here.'

'We're just friends. What's the problem?'

'You're the problem.'

'I haven't done anything wrong.'

'Helen and Hannah are younger than you are.'

'Only a few years,' Rio argued.

'You're testing my patience,' Ernie said. 'You're sixteen next month and you're an adolescent. The age gap between you and my daughters is vast. They're still children,' Ernie said. Rio half smiled. Beneath his surprise, he was arrogant. 'Don't smirk at me, Rio. Taking the piss out of me would be a huge mistake.'

'I'm not smirking,' Rio said, smirking.

'You're an idiot. Now listen to me very carefully.' Ernie kept the anger out of his voice, but his eyes told a different story. They bored through his mind to the back of his head. 'I told you very politely to leave my daughter alone, and you told me to take a chill-pill. That's very disrespectful and I won't tolerate being disrespected.'

'It's just a saying. I didn't mean anything insulting by it.' Rio snorted a laugh and grinned. He shrugged. 'Like I said, we're just friends. There's nothing to worry about, Ernie.'

'I'll decide what I worry about and if it's to do with my daughter, then I'm plenty worried,' Ernie said. 'And if you ever call me Ernie again, I'll break your nose.'

'Wow, you really do need to chill. You've gone all gangsta on me,' Rio said, smirking again. 'Are you threatening me, Mr Metcalfe?' he asked. 'Because if you are, I'll be informing my teachers and my parents and probably the police would have to be involved.'

'I don't make threats, Rio,' Ernie said quietly.

'I think I'll go to school now, if you don't mind moving the fuck out of my way?'

Ernie punched him hard in the chest. The impact was short, sharp, and devastating. Rio's eyes bulged from his head and he staggered backwards, gasping as the wind was knocked from his lungs. Ernie closed the gap between them quickly, moving without effort.

'I don't make threats and it's clear you don't listen, anyway.' He kicked Rio between the legs, making the boy squeal like a pig. 'Is that chilled enough for you?'

Rio wanted to scream for help but he was winded badly and couldn't catch his breath. Ernie grabbed the boy by his genitals and squeezed hard. Rio folded in half and gasped for air. Tears streamed from his eyes. His hands clawed at Ernie's face, but he couldn't stop the agonising hold he had on him. Ernie pushed him against a tree.

'You were staring at your phone while you were walking,' Ernie whispered in his ear. 'Let's see what you were looking at, shall we?'

Ernie twisted Rio's genitals and bent down to pick up his phone. The screen lit up, and Ernie saw the message thread. Helen Metcalfe was the recipient.

'Look here,' Ernie said. 'How ironic is that?'

'Let go of me,' Rio gasped. 'Give me my phone!'

'Let's see what you were messaging my thirteen-year-old daughter.' Ernie held the phone in one hand and kept Rio's testicles in the other. 'Have you kissed anyone with your mouth open yet?' Ernie read from the screen. His eyes narrowed and his face flushed read. 'I can teach you how.' Ernie put the phone into his pocket. 'She's a thirteen-year-old child, so that makes you a paedophile.' His expression was unchanged as he butted Rio hard. There was a sickening crunch. He squeezed his genitals harder again. 'I warned you to leave her alone, but you wouldn't listen.'

The colour drained from Rio's face. Tears ran from his eyes and blood ran from both nostrils. His mouth opened, but no words came out, just desperate gasps. Saliva mixed with blood and ran from his chin. Ernie pushed his chin upward, hard and fast. He felt the boy's skull hit the tree trunk and Rio's eyes rolled backwards into his head. His body went limp and crumpled at the knees. Ernie reached around his body and grabbed his belt, lifting him into the air. He tossed Rio into the stream like a rag doll and the boy landed in the shallow water, face down. Blood from his nose and the wound on his scalp coloured the crystal-clear water red. Ernie stepped towards the water to finish him off, but he heard voices from further down the path. A group of girls was approaching. He took one last glance at Rio before slipping into the trees and skirting his way back to the road. The boy was flapping about and his face was submerged. It wasn't ideal, but there was nothing more he could do for now.

He took the SIM card from Rio's phone and snapped it, dropping the Samsung down a grid at the side of the road. No one would find it there and he would delete the message thread from Helen's phone when he got home. Her replies to Rio's questions had not made pleasant reading for a doting dad and were not appropriate for a thirteen-year-old. She had said she wanted to learn how to kiss with her mouth open. He hadn't felt so disappointed since he'd found Naomi cheating, and that was three years ago.

The little slut was just like her mother.

Chapter 5

Chod was parking the car when he heard the shotgun blast from the upstairs bedroom. Richard was opening the kitchen door to check outside in the back garden. Both of them were stunned for a moment. Alan had cried out, but a terrifying silence followed it. The detectives ran to help him and reached the bottom of the stairs at the same time. Chod took the first three stairs in one leap. Richard was right behind him. Neither man gave a second thought to their own safety. There could have been a gunman waiting for them, but their superior officer, and friend, was upstairs in mortal danger.

'Armed police!' Chod shouted in the hope a gunman would flee or surrender.

When they reached the landing, they could see Alan was lying on his back, his feet in the bedroom, head and torso on the landing. He was still and silent, his face a bloody mess.

'Armed police,' he called again. 'Step out of the bedroom with your hands up.'

Chod crept along the wall, his back to the plaster. He reached the door and peered around the frame. He could see the shotgun was sitting on a bedside table, fastened to a frame of some kind. There was no gunman and no sign of Kim.

'It was a booby trap,' Chod said, kneeling next to Alan. 'Get on the comms and tell them we have an officer down.' He felt for a pulse in the neck. It was weak, but it was there. Alan was breathing, but his chest was making a hissing sound. 'He's got a punctured lung,' Chod said. He ran into the bathroom and grabbed two towels before returning. 'Hang in there, Alan,' he said, pressing one of the towels to a perforated wound in his chest. 'Richard is on the comms. An ambulance is on the way. Can you hear me?'

There was no response. His eyelids flickered but didn't open.

'Come on, Alan. Stop fooling around,' he muttered, trying to get a response. 'If you want some time off, book it,' he said, stemming the bleeding. 'There's no need for all the dramatics. This is just a scratch.' Alan remained unresponsive. 'A few holes in your chest aren't going to impress anyone. It's a good performance, but you're not fooling me.' No reply. 'Do you remember that guy from Llangefni called Tetley? He got blasted in the chest, just like this. You said he had more perforations than a teabag and we all called him Tetley after that.' Nothing. 'Come on, Alan. Give us a smile.'

'ARU and paramedics are on the way,' Richard said. 'How is he?'

'Fucked,' Chod said. 'He has way too many holes in him.'

'Don't let him hear you saying that,' Richard said, shaking his head.

'I think he probably knows already,' Chod said. 'There's blood coming from everywhere.'

'Check for where he's bleeding the most,' Richard said, kneeling next to Alan's head. 'This neck wound is a priority. We need more towels.'

'There's a cupboard next to the bathroom,' Chod said, pointing.

Richard walked across the landing and opened the door. There were no towels. That was odd. He grabbed a stack of clean sheets and ran back to Alan.

'Has he said anything or moved?' Richard asked. Chod shook his head and took a sheet from him. He pressed it to the neck wound, and the cotton turned blood red instantly. 'He's going to bleed out if we don't stop the bleeding.'

'I can't see where he's injured,' Chod said, panicking. 'There's too much blood everywhere. Find some scissors so we can cut his clothes off.' Richard ran back to the bathroom. 'Can you hear me, Alan?' Chod asked, pressing the sheet to a leg wound. He wrapped it around the thigh and tied it as tightly as he could. The sheet on his neck was saturated with blood already. He tore a strip from another sheet and replaced it with a clean piece.

'Where's the fucking ambulance?' he shouted.

Richard returned with a pair of hairdressing snippers. He began cutting Alan's sleeves in half. There were pellet holes in both biceps and a chunk of the left forearm was missing. The wound was gaping and bleeding heavily. They cut a thick strip of towel and tied it around the forearm, working quickly together to slow the bleeding.

'Let's see his chest and abdomen,' Chod said, checking his legs with his hands. 'The left leg feels the wettest,' he added. Richard snipped the shirt down the middle. Alan had taken most of the blast to his chest. 'Look at the state of you. You've got more holes in you than United's defence,' Chod said to Alan, who was an avid Manchester United fan. 'What, no comeback?' Chod asked. There was no response to the jibe. 'You won't be able to walk through an airport scanner anymore without setting off the metal detectors.' Alan didn't move, smile, or laugh. There was no response at all. 'And we've fucked up Kim's bedding supplies. She'll have a fit when she sees how much washing she's got to do.' Alan didn't flinch, not so much as a twitch. 'You're going to be in for a real earbashing,' he said. 'Are you listening to me?'

The air hissed from his chest, his breathing becoming shallow.

'Put some pressure on here while I cut his trousers,' Richard said. He cut the trousers from the ankle to the knee first. There were two pellet wounds, but the bleeding wasn't profuse. Then he cut from the knee to the hip. The left thigh was gushing from half a dozen wounds. 'We need to wrap this up tightly,' he said, cutting a sheet in half. The sound of sirens approaching reached them. 'Help is on the way,' Richard said loudly. 'Alan. Can you hear me?'

There was no response. They heard the Armed Response Unit shouting and checking the ground floor and the sound of boots on the stairs.

'Is it clear up here?'

'Yes,' Chod said. 'The weapon's in there. It was a booby trap.'

Two armed officers went into the bedroom and checked the weapon and the rest of the room. They called it clear for the paramedics to come up.

The paramedics appeared on the landing. Chod and Richard stood up and stepped back to allow them access. Two more ambulance men arrived.

'We'll take over, gents. You've done a great job. Leave us to it,' one of them said.

'Has he spoken at all?' another asked, checking his pulse.

'He asked where the ambulance was and what was taking you so long.' The ambulance man took no notice of the jibe.

'Seriously?'

'No,' Chod said. 'He hasn't spoken. Not a word.'

'What the hell happened?'

'DI Davies didn't show up for work this morning, so we came to see what was wrong and the gaffer walked into a booby trap,' Richard said.

'Bastards,' one of the medics said. 'And what happened to the DI?'

'We haven't got a clue,' Chod said. 'But we're going to find out.'

Chapter 6

Rio felt himself being lifted, and then he felt like he was choking. His senses were reeling as water was expelled from his lungs. A blinding pain was pulsing in his head and his testicles felt like they were being crushed in a vice. He vomited, the bile burning his throat. Voices reached him. They were calling his name. He opened his eyes and looked into the face of his PE teacher, Mr McDonald. Everything sounded muffled, as if he was still underwater. Rio had the sensation of being carried and he saw clouds floating against a vivid blue sky. His nose hurt and his head was throbbing. He felt water run from his ear holes and his hearing returned with a pop. Full volume was restored.

'Can you hear me, Rio?' the teacher asked. He asked him again, louder this time. Rio nodded and coughed stream water onto his chest. He was beginning to shiver from the cold and shock was setting in.

'Is he okay, sir?' a girl's voice asked. She sounded concerned.

'He is thanks to you girls,' the teacher said. 'You got to him just in time. He's got a nasty cut on the back of his head and a bloody nose. Did you see what happened?'

'No. We heard someone spluttering and splashing about. When we looked where the noise was coming from, we saw him in the stream. He kept trying to get up, but it was too slippery, and he kept falling over.'

'That's probably how he banged his head and broke his nose,' another girl said. Rio wanted to argue, but he didn't have the energy. 'He was falling about all over the place,' she added.

'Goodness knows what happened to him. He's lucky you girls came along when you did. There's an ambulance on the way,' another teacher said. Rio recognised the voice; it belonged to the head teacher, Miss Jenkins. 'You girls have saved his life. Well done to all of you.' She nodded patronisingly, smiling at each one of them in turn. 'Now, we need to get to the bottom of what happened.' Her expression became stern. 'How did he get into the water?' The girls shrugged and shook their heads.

'We didn't see him fall in, miss,' the first said.

'He was already splashing about when we saw him,' another said.

'Was he clowning around with any other boys?' the head asked suspiciously. Her eyes narrowed, searching for lies. 'Did you see him fall in?'

'No, miss,' one of them answered. Rio could see four faces he recognised. They were in the year above him studying for A-levels. Two of them were fit and two of them were mega-fit, but they were all out of his league and had boyfriends with cars. One of their boyfriends was in his twenties and drove a Porsche. Way out of his league. 'When we got there, he fell forward and was lying face down in the middle of the stream. When he lifted his head up, there was blood all over his face. He kept trying to get up but he couldn't and then he fell backwards and cracked his head again.'

'Was he near the bank?' the head asked.

'No. He was in the deeper water.'

'In the middle of the stream?' Miss Jenkins asked. 'Are you sure?'

'Yes, miss.'

'So, he couldn't have slipped down the bank and rolled in?' she asked, frowning.

'No, miss. He was in the middle.'

'Did you see anyone else around?'

'No. There was no one else there, miss.'

'And you're not covering for any of his silly friends?' the head asked. The girls shook their heads.

'I'll put him down here,' Mr McDonald said.

The gym teacher had tired of carrying him and put him down on a bench, trying to get his breath back. Rio was calming down. The panic had passed and his breathing was returning to normal. His hands were blue with cold and another teacher brought a thermal wrap and dry shoes and socks from the lost property. Another had a pair of mittens that had been left behind and never reclaimed. They stripped his shoes and socks. Rio wiggled his fingers and toes to get his circulation going. The wrap made him feel warmer but his clothes were saturated and cold. His teeth chattered and his hands were shaking. They brought him a cup of weak tea. He sipped it and felt embarrassed in front of the older girls.

'You should get out of those wet clothes,' the head said.

'I'll be fine,' Rio muttered. There was no way he was stripping off in front of this crowd. The head caught his glance at the girls.

'You should be very grateful to these young ladies,' Miss Jenkins said.

'I am. Thank you very much.' Rio nodded that he was. Miss Jenkins thanked them and told them to go to their classes.

'The ambulance will be here soon. How are you feeling?' she asked him.

'Cold and a bit shaken,' Rio said.

'I'm not surprised. You almost drowned. Rio, what on Earth were you doing in the stream?' the head asked. 'Did you fall?'

'No.'

'No?'

'I was thrown in, miss.'

'Thrown in?' she repeated, surprised. 'Good heavens. Thrown into the stream on purpose?'

'Yes. I was attacked.'

'Goodness gracious me. Tell me what happened.'

'I was just walking along the path and a man stepped out from behind a tree and attacked me,' Rio said. He coughed up phlegm and more water.

'Get it all up, son,' Mr McDonald said. He patted him on the back.

'My bollocks feel like they're on fire, sir,' Rio said, lowering his voice.

'What did you just say?' Miss Jenkins asked, shocked.

'My balls are hurting me, miss,' Rio said. 'He grabbed me and twisted my balls.'

'Good heavens. Why did he do that?'

'He's fucking nuts.'

'Don't use that language please,' the head said, shocked.

'Sorry, miss,' Rio said. 'But he is nuts.'

'Who, exactly is, nuts?'

'The bloke who attacked me. Mr Metcalfe.'

'I understand you think he's a madman but are you saying that you were assaulted by someone you know?'

'Sort of. Yes, miss.'

'Was it someone from our school?'

'No, miss,' Rio said, dithering. 'It was a man called Ernie Metcalfe.'

'You're sure you know who it was?'

'Yes, miss.'

'I'll call the police immediately. He could be around here waiting for someone else to attack.'

'I'll go and check,' Mr McDonald said.

'I don't think he's looking for anyone else, miss,' Rio said. 'He was waiting for me.'

'I don't follow.'

'I don't know him but I know who he is,' Rio said. 'His name is Metcalfe. I think his first name is Ernest.'

'How do you know him?' Miss Jenkins asked, confused.

'I don't know him,' Rio said. 'I'm friends with his daughter Helen on Facebook.'

'Why on Earth did he attack you?'

'I don't know, miss,' Rio said. 'He jumped out from behind a tree and grabbed my penis and I slapped his hand away and he just attacked me for nothing. But he kept trying to grab my penis. I think he's a perv.'

'Did he say anything to you?'

'He squeezed my balls really hard. I think I'll be bruised down there, miss,' he added. 'Maybe he's a paedo.'

'I don't know what the world is coming to,' Miss Jenkins said, dialling triple nine. 'But I promise you, he won't get away with this. I'll have him locked up for a long time.'

Chapter 7

Pamela Stone headed towards the house on the Gorad Road and was accompanied by her assistant, Rob Wilkinson, and every available member of her team. They were already stretched, so two photographers had been drafted in from a sister company in Manchester. News of the attack on two senior detectives on Anglesey had reached the top echelons of other forces, and the repercussions were only just beginning to be felt.

Offers of help with manpower and resources were pouring in from neighbouring forces. Such attacks on police offers were incredibly rare and were usually terrorist related or the work of a serious crime gang seeking revenge. If either were responsible, it wouldn't be contained within the North Wales Police. Forces across the country would be alerted to hunt for the perpetrators. Every detective that could be mobilised had been seconded to the Holyhead MIT.

The Chief Constable, Diane Warburton, was less than two years into her role and she had flown back from a meeting in London to oversee the investigation with her assistant chief constable, Bill Armstrong. The ACC was new to the post, and this was his first major incident. Ironically, the attack had taken out two of his best detectives and he was trying to wrestle control. He was on the scene, which was chaotic.

Pamela and her team made their way slowly through the cordon in four vehicles. Concerned onlookers and the first responders from the press were already becoming a nuisance, hindering access in and out of the narrow street.

'Look at these people just standing in the road. I'm going to run someone over,' Rob said, weaving through groups of people who appeared to be oblivious to them. He beeped the horn to alert a group of men and woman who carried cameras and sound booms. 'Get out of the way!' he shouted through the window. 'Bloody idiots,' he mumbled as they parted reluctantly.

'Temper, temper,' Pamela said, waving at one of the photographers. 'Let's not upset the locals before we've even arrived.'

'I think this is going to be a nightmare,' Rob said. He pointed to a space where they could park. 'It looks like every policeman and his dog are here.'

'It's the typical overreaction we should expect when two of their own are attacked. It's bound to happen,' Pamela said. She turned to the team in the back of the vehicle. 'We treat this like every other case. We process the scene and analyse what we find. The fact it's Alan Williams and Kim Davies who are the victims can't influence us one way or the other. The evidence is what it is, no matter who the victims are.'

'There will be a different level of expectation. They're going to be looking for answers pronto,' Rob said, shaking his head. 'Nothing about this is going to be like any other case. Not a chance.'

'Let's be positive, shall we?' Pamela said.

'Always. Never a cloud will darken my day.' Rob shook his head. 'I couldn't smile any wider if I tried,' he added, grinning.

'Don't be a knob,' Pamela said.

'Sorry,' Rob muttered.

'Let's go and find some answers.'

They exited the vehicle and collected their kit from the back of the van. The press was excited by their arrival. Cameras flashed and a barrage of questions was hurled at them.

'Is this a murder investigation?'

'What are you looking for, a body?'

'Has there been any ransom demands?'

'Is this revenge for Operation Thor?'

'See what I mean,' Rob said, grabbing a case of equipment and a pair of overshoes. 'I haven't put my shoes on yet and they want answers.'

'The press will be all over this,' Pamela said, scanning the throng of reporters. 'I can't see anyone from the nationals here yet. They're all locals. It won't be long before the big dogs get here and then things could turn nasty.'

'This is going to be big news.'

'Too big for the Anglesey Mail and the Daily Post.' DS Lewis approached them through a throng of uniformed officers. Pamela spotted him. 'Hello, Richard.'

'Hello. I'm glad you're here,' Richard said. 'How are you both?'

'We're fine,' Pamela said. 'Any news on Kim?'

'Nothing,' Richard said. 'Her car is in the garage, but she's missing. Still, it's early days yet. She might turn up.'

'Unlikely,' Pamela said.

'Sorry?' Richard said.

'People of Kim's age don't just turn up,' Pamela said. 'Young children or dementia sufferers turn up, not detective inspectors.'

'Oh, I agree with you,' Richard said. 'We haven't had a ransom demand, which tells me she's already dead but until we find her…'

'You said, "let's try to be positive",' Rob said, sarcastically. Pamela shot him a withering glance. 'I know what you're about to say. I'll try not to be a knob.'

'Try harder.' She turned back to Richard. 'And how's Alan?' Pamela asked.

'Someone rigged a Mossberg to the door handle. He walked into two barrels of shot,' Richard said. 'Most of it hit him in the chest. Twelve inches higher and it would have blown his head off. It's touch and go. He lost a lot of blood.' Richard gestured to the house. 'We have a new ACC on the scene, Bill Armstrong. Do you know him?'

'He was with GMP, wasn't he?' Pamela asked. 'Working in the gangs unit.'

'That's him,' Richard said. 'He's not been around long, but he's a decent bloke and he seems to be in charge, which is good. He's coming over as cool, calm, and collected while everyone else seems to be running around like headless chickens in a barn fire. We don't know who's going to be the SIO yet, but it will probably be a DCI or above from a different force but there's no doubt who'll be pulling the strings. Diane Warburton will be calling the shots.'

'That makes sense,' Pamela said.

'So, until we get an SIO, whatever you need to do, ask me for authorisation and I'll say yes, no matter what the cost.' He shrugged and lowered his voice. 'What I'm saying is, don't bother asking me, just get on with it. There's no budget on this until we're told otherwise. We just need answers. Test everything and anything that will put us closer to whoever has Kim.'

'We understand,' Pamela said. 'Let's get on with it, shall we?'

Chapter 8

Sergeants Bob Dewhurst and April Byfelt were waiting until Rio's parents had arrived before they could speak to him about the alleged assault in detail. An initial report had been made at the school by a constable from Beaumaris. It wasn't clear to him if the injuries had been caused by the boy falling over numerous times in the Dingle or if an assault on a minor had occurred and that could be considered as a sexual assault.

On any other day, Rio would have been interviewed by detectives, but there weren't any available, so experienced uniformed sergeants were sent. Bob ran a quick record check on Ernest Metcalfe and found out he was an ex-serviceman and had been an RAF police officer. He was a widower with three young daughters, and he remembered him losing his wife in a car crash a few years earlier. There was talk of an affair or a love triangle, which resulted in her psycho lover killing his wife and kids; he was serving a full-life term and would never be released. Metcalfe was as clean as a whistle.

They needed to interview the victim, weigh up the evidence, and make a call. If there were any issues and the complaint against

Metcalfe was genuine, a detective could dig deeper when the opportunity arose. That was the best they could do for now. All detective resources had been allocated to find Kim Davies and whoever set the booby trap.

When they arrived at the hospital, they'd enquired about Alan and were told was he was in surgery and no news was good news, but a consultant Bob had known for years said it didn't look good.

'Rio Wood's parents are here,' the ward sister said. 'You can have five minutes with him, but the doctor doesn't want him "interrogated", was the word he used.'

'We call it interviewing,' Bob said.

'You can call it whatever you like. I'm just repeating what he said. Don't shoot the messenger. You have five minutes, remember.'

'Thank you,' Bob said. 'We'll try not to cause any bruises, but if we do have to get heavy, he's in the right place.' The sister left, laughing to herself. 'Shall we?' He gestured for April to go first.

'Let me do the talking,' April said.

'What does that mean?'

'You're a clumsy bastard and he's fifteen and badly shaken,' April said.

'Ah, I see,' Bob said.

'You know it makes sense.'

'I resemble that comment.' Bob chuckled and nodded in agreement.

They knocked on the door and walked into the room. Rio Woods was sitting up in bed. His eyes were blackening and his nose was purple and swollen. A bandage had been wrapped around his head, pinning his ears to his scalp. There were two females and a male sitting around the bed. 'I'm Sergeant Byfelt and this is Sergeant Dewhurst. We're here to ask you some questions about what happened to you earlier. If you feel up to it?'

'Before he answers any questions, has he been arrested?' a female sitting by the window asked.

'I'm sorry,' April said.

'Don't be sorry, just tell us you've arrested that paedophile and locked him up,' Miss Jenkins said. She folded her arms across her chest. The uniformed officers exchanged glances. 'Has he been arrested?'

'Has who been arrested?' Bob asked, irritated by the tone she'd used to pose the question.

'Ernest Metcalfe,' the woman said. 'Rio knows who attacked him and we told the police officer who came to school what the attacker's name is. Has he been arrested?'

'No arrests have been made yet. And may I ask who you are?' Bob asked, politely.

'Cerris Jenkins. Head teacher.'

'I see,' Bob said, smiling. 'Are you Rio's mum?' Bob asked the second female. She nodded.

'I'm Wendy.'

'And you're Rio's dad?' Bob asked the male.

'He is when it suits him,' Wendy jumped in before he could answer. 'When he's not pissed out of his brains in the Dublin Packet.'

'The Dublin's been closed for two years.'

'That hasn't stopped you,' Wendy said. 'He spends every penny he has on ale and pisses it all up the wall. Can't call himself a father. He couldn't spell it.'

'Why don't you stop talking through your arse and give your mouth a chance to speak,' the man snapped. He shook his head. 'I'm Jimmy. Rio's dad.'

'Now we've cleared up who's who, can we ask you to leave us with Rio and his parents please?' April said to Cerris. She looked offended. 'We appreciate you're concerned for Rio, but he's safe now and we'll take over from here.' Cerris stood up and blushed red, her lips tight and narrow like a slit in a paper bag.

'I don't know what you're waiting for,' she said. 'Rio has identified his attacker. This is a serious sexual assault, and the perpetrator is still walking the streets. The man is a danger to the public.'

'If that's the case, he'll be arrested, but we need to speak to Rio to confirm the facts before we do anything,' Bob said, opening the door.

'You're wasting time,' Miss Jenkins said.

'It's called running an investigation,' Bob said. He smiled and nodded towards the door. 'So, if you don't mind, you're hampering our enquiries.'

'I'm hampering the police now, am I?'

'Yes. We need to question Rio in the presence of his parents and you're holding up the interview,' Bob said. 'When I went to school, that was the definition of hampering. Look it up when you get back to your desk,' he joked.

'Well, I don't think I've been so insulted in all my life,' Miss Jenkins said, storming towards the door, nose in the air.

'It was joke,' Bob said.

'Well, your joke wasn't funny and there's a time and a place to be a comedian and this isn't the time or the place,' Miss Jenkins ranted. 'I'll be speaking to the Assistant Chief Constable. He's a governor of our school. Your attitude is a disgrace.'

'I know Bill Armstrong very well and he'll probably agree with you about my comedic timing, however I still need you to leave.' Miss Jenkins walked out of the door in a puff of white linen and talcum powder. Bob nodded and smiled, closing the door behind her. 'I haven't been told off like that since school,' he said, turning back to the Woods family. 'Is she always like that?' he asked Rio.

'Most of the time,' Rio answered.

'Right, let's get going,' Bob said. 'Sergeant Byfelt is going to ask you some questions. We need you to answer them in as much detail as you can remember, okay?'

'Yes,' Rio answered.

'You can call me April,' she said.

'Okay,' Rio said, nodding. Rio looked April up and down like she was about to perform in a pole dancing bar. Bob spotted the lust in his eyes. April was a very pretty woman, and Rio Wood was a horny teenage boy. An attractive policewoman in uniform with handcuffs on her belt was fantasy material. 'I'll do my best.'

'Rio, we can see your cuts and bruises and it's obvious you've been injured,' April said. 'The officer who spoke to you at the school said you were in the stream when they found you and that you fell forwards onto your face?'

'Yes. I think so,' Rio said, nodding. 'It's all a bit blurry. He hit my head against a tree and head-butted me before he threw me into the Dingle.'

'Okay,' April said. 'So, you were already hurt before you went into the water?'

'Yes.'

'Were you bleeding before you went into the water?'

'Yes.'

'Tell me where?'

'The back of my head where he pushed me against the tree and my nose where he head-butted me,' Rio said.

'Your injuries are clear to see. What we need to do now is establish who attacked you and why,' April said.

'I understand,' Rio said, nodding.

'Who attacked you?'

'Ernest Metcalfe.'

'And how do you know this man?'

'I'm friends with his daughter on social media.'

'You've never met him in person?'

'No.'

'Have you had any communication with him before today?'

'No,' Rio blinked as he answered.

'Tell us what happened from when you first saw Ernest Metcalfe,' April said. 'Where were you?'

'I was on the path on the way to school,' Rio said. 'We always cut through the Dingle.'

'You said 'we' but you were alone?'

'Yes. My mates had run ahead.'

'They ran ahead and left you?'

'Yes.'

'Why was that?'

'They were chasing Brian Mullins,' Rio said, nodding as if it was normal. 'He's a proper knobhead. We always chase him on the way to school.'

'I see. Then what happened?'

'He jumped out from behind a tree and tried to grab my penis,' Rio said. He looked at his mum and then his dad. They looked on concerned for their son. 'So, I slapped his hand away.'

'Dirty pervert,' Wendy said, shaking her head.

'He went nuts on me. He must be mental.'

'Did he say anything to you?' April asked.

'He said something about recognising me from Facebook, I think.'

'Facebook?'

'Yes. It's all a bit blurry, but he mentioned seeing pictures of me on Helen's feed,' Rio said.

'He said what exactly?' April asked. Rio looked down at his hands. 'It's very important we get the exact sequence of events.'

'I can't remember,' Rio said, blushing.

'Tell me roughly what he said?'

'Something about images on Facebook.'

'So, he said, "I've seen you on Facebook" or "I've seen pictures of you on Facebook"?' April asked, studying his discomfort with the question.

'Something like that,' Rio said, nodding.

'Did he say that before he attacked you or during the attack?' April asked.

'At the same time,' Rio said, blushing.

'I'm confused. Let me get this straight in my mind's eye,' Bob interrupted. April rolled her eyes and took a deep breath. He was incapable of keeping quiet for long. 'Your attacker stepped out of the trees and made a grab for your penis, simultaneously saying he had seen pictures of you on his daughter's Facebook?'

'Yes.' Rio reddened a little. He shrugged. 'He must have been looking at her profile page and seen pictures of me.'

'We'll need to see those pictures,' Bob said.

'I don't think they're there anymore,' Rio said. 'She must have taken them down.'

'That's handy,' Bob said, scrutinising Rio. 'Why would he mention these mysterious images?'

'I reckon he's been perving over me.' Rio made a wanking motion with his right hand. 'You know what I mean. Keeping the images in the wank bank.' Rio tapped his temple with his forefinger. 'I bet he's a massive paedo.'

'I'll kill him,' Jimmy said. 'Wait until I get my hands on him.'

'You'll have to wait in the queue,' Wendy said angrily. 'I'm not having some old perv wanking over my boy. I'll kill him!'

'No one is going to kill anyone,' April said. 'Let's keep calm regardless of how distressing it may sound.'

'He needs locking up,' Jimmy said. 'Fucking pervert.'

'Has he ever contacted you on social media before?' Bob asked.

'No.' Rio shook his head. 'I don't think so.'

'You don't think so?' Bob asked. 'I think you would remember if he had contacted you, don't you?'

'My head's a bit foggy,' Rio said, grimacing.

'How do you think he knows which school you go to?' Bob asked.

'He must have asked Helen.'

'His daughter?'

'Yes.'

'Okay. Helen is your friend?' Bob asked.

'Yes,' Rio said.

'Does she go to school with you?'

'No. She goes to Bodedern. Her dad wants her to be able to speak Welsh,' Rio said.

'How do you know Helen?'

'I know her from Facebook. We have mutual friends. That's how we got talking.'

'How long have you been talking to her?'

'A couple of months or so.'

'Did you add her as a friend, or did she add you?' Bob asked. April raised an eyebrow in surprise and suppressed a smile.

'Why does that matter?' Rio said defensively.

'It matters to her father,' Bob said. 'She's very young. And if you don't see why it matters, that concerns me.' Rio looked embarrassed but didn't speak. Bob raised his eyebrows and lowered his tone. 'How old is she?' Bob asked.

'I'm not sure,' Rio lied. He blushed.

'I'm sure you do.'

'I'm not sure. She's just a mate.'

'Is she younger than you?' Bob pushed.

'Yes. I think so, but I'm not certain.'

'What year is she in at school?' April asked, frowning.

'She's below me,' Rio said, blushing. 'I'm not sure though.'

'She's actually thirteen,' Bob said, nodding.

'Okay. So what?'

'And you're fifteen, going on sixteen?' Bob asked.

'What are you getting at?' Wendy Woods asked. 'I don't like your tone.'

'I'm not getting at anything,' Bob said. 'I'm trying to establish the relationship between your son and his attacker.'

'What relationship?' Jimmy said. 'He's told you he doesn't know him, but he knows who he is.'

'I don't see why you're asking him these questions?' Wendy said.

'Unprovoked attacks of this nature are rare,' April said. 'There's usually a trigger if the victim is known to the attacker. We're trying to establish the motive behind the attack.'

'He's a bender with a thing for young lads,' Jimmy Woods said shrugging. 'He's attacked our Rio and tried grabbing his cock. The doctor said his testicles are bruised. What more evidence of the motive do you need?'

'Evidence is in short supply at the moment,' Bob said. 'There are witnesses who saw Rio falling over a number of times, banging his face and the back of his head. We need as much evidence as is physically possible to arrest this man. Calling him a bender isn't going to get us a warrant.'

'I understand that,' Jimmy said. 'Can't you remember anything specific he said to you, son?' Rio shook his head.

'Do you think the attack was sexually motivated?' Bob asked Rio. Rio blushed again, but didn't answer. 'I'm struggling here.'

'I can't see what you're struggling with,' Jimmy said angrily. 'He's a fucking bender.'

'Let me explain my problem to you,' Bob said.

'Go on,' Jimmy said.

'Ernest Metcalfe is a family man with three daughters' – Bob paused – 'He's ex-army and a decorated ex-RAF police officer.' He paused again. 'His record is squeaky clean and you want me to believe that suddenly he's become a sexual predator with a penchant for teenage boys?' Bob shook his head and sighed. 'I just don't see that being the truth.'

'I've known a few blokes who turned out to be on the other bus,' Jimmy said, frowning. 'They don't all have paedo tattooed on their foreheads.'

'There's a huge gulf between someone being privately attracted to the opposite sex and an attack on a teenage boy,' Bob said. 'My experience with these types of attacks is that there's a piece of the jigsaw missing.'

'I don't like your tone,' Wendy snapped. 'Our Rio has been attacked, head-butted, and tossed into a river, and his balls are black and blue. He nearly drowned and you're here grilling him while he's lying in a hospital bed. How the fuck does that work?'

'He's the fucking victim here,' Jimmy added.

'We're not questioning the fact that an assault has occurred, but we're exploring the motivation behind it,' April interrupted, trying to keep things on an even keel. 'We have to ask questions and explore all the possible reasons for it. No one is saying Rio is anything but an innocent victim here,' she added. She glared at Bob. 'Are they, Bob?'

'Oh no. Heaven forbid,' Bob said, shaking his head. 'It's clear from his injuries he's been assaulted, but what isn't clear is why.'

'That's not our problem,' Wendy said. 'He's clearly a fucking lunatic with sexual issues. Our Rio is the victim here.'

'I didn't mean to imply Rio might be being economical with the truth,' Bob said, shaking his head. 'Heaven forbid.'

'Economical with the truth. Are you taking the piss?' Jimmy asked. 'Because it sounds like it to me.'

'I'm stating the facts as I see them,' Bob said. 'My professional curiosity tells me something is missing.'

'The facts are that my son has been assaulted by a bender and if you don't sort it, I know people who will.'

'You need to wind your neck in, Jimmy, before you get yourself into trouble,' Bob said, smiling thinly. 'Talk like that will get you arrested. Calm down for a minute and look at this objectively. Take the emotion out of the situation for two minutes and try to see the situation with clarity,' Bob said.

He looked at both parents. They sat back and listened.

'Let's go back to square one and sum up what Rio's saying, shall we?' Bob said. Wendy and Jimmy nodded and relaxed a little. 'Rio was walking to school, minding his own business when Mr Metcalfe, a family man with three daughters under the age of fourteen, jumps out from behind a tree, announcing that he's seen pictures of Rio on his daughter's Facebook page. Then he grabbed his genitals, head-butted him, and threw him into the stream. For no apparent reason,' Bob said. Looking from one parent to the other. 'I can accept an assault has taken place. There's absolutely no excuse for assaulting Rio and causing him bodily harm, but I cannot fathom what has provoked this attack and what Rio has said makes no sense.' Bob held up his hands to keep the peace.

'Don't jump down my throat. Those are the facts. Either Mr Metcalfe has had a mental breakdown or he's a very dangerous predator, who has kept his activities a secret for decades. I have the feeling something is missing from this story, don't you?'

'It does sound a bit odd when you look at it like that,' Jimmy said. He looked at Rio, but his son didn't meet his gaze.

'That's typical of you,' Wendy said. 'You never back him up. Why don't you believe what your own son's saying?'

'Like when he said he had nothing to do with smashing up Pissy-Liz's car but we found the number plate under his bed?' Jimmy snapped at Wendy. 'He's not exactly been the arc angel of Anglesey and he doesn't know the truth from his arsehole!'

'Cheers, Dad,' Rio said, blushing again. 'Thanks for your support when I need it.'

'You're such a wanker, Jimmy,' Wendy said, raising her voice. 'Ali-Bach gave him that number plate. He didn't know where it had come from.'

'Oh yes. I forgot he's collected number plates since he was a toddler,' Jimmy said. 'Or is he just a lying bastard on occasions?'

'You never believe anything I say,' Rio shouted at his father.

'You told me Marc Almond visited the school during a music lesson on his way to play a concert at the Driftwood,' Jimmy said. 'Some of my mates still go on about that today. They booked taxis to take us to Trearddur Bay.'

'For fuck's sake,' Wendy said. 'He was thirteen. He doesn't even know who Marc Almond is. He found one of your old singles and wanted to impress you.'

'It's still a fucking lie,' Jimmy said, shrugging.

'We're going down the wrong track here. Calm down, both of you. It's not a case of believing him,' Bob said. 'I think something is missing from this story, don't you?'

Jimmy and Wendy exchanged glances. There was doubt in their eyes.

'Have you left something out?' Jimmy asked his son. Rio blushed again, darker this time. 'Because if you're lying about this, I'll tan your backside.'

'Fuck off, Dad,' Rio said angrily. 'I haven't seen you for weeks and you couldn't tan your shoes.'

'Don't you threaten my son,' Wendy snapped, standing up and leaning over Rio. 'I'll break your neck before you lay a hand on him. You're a waste of space, you useless pisspot.'

'You're a fine one talking,' Jimmy said. He snorted and pointed at Wendy. 'Whiskey Wendy they call her in the Branch.'

'That's enough,' April said, stepping in. 'Making threats and insulting each other is only going to end up with you both being charged. For the sake of your son, I need you to calm down and behave like reasonable adults.'

'I'm out of here,' Jimmy said, marching to the door. 'Ungrateful bastards. I came here to make sure you were okay,' he said turning to Rio. 'And this is the thanks I get.'

'I'm okay thanks, Dad, so you can fuck off again now,' Rio shouted. 'I'll see you in another six weeks when you need a borrow from Mum.'

'I wouldn't hold your breath,' Jimmy said, slamming the door open. 'I'd rather shove wasps up my arse than ask her for a penny.' He stepped out and slammed the door closed behind him.

There was an embarrassing silence. April shook her head in despair.

'That's your fault,' Wendy said, pointing at Bob. 'You caused that. You with your stupid questions. Trying to make our Rio look like a liar.'

'No one is saying Rio is a liar,' April said, shaking her head. 'We're trying to get to the root cause of the assault. We've heard what Rio has had to say. Now we'll go speak to Ernest Metcalfe.' She stood next to Bob and nudged him. Bob opened the door and waited. 'Obviously, we need to investigate what's happened to Rio. Leave it with us. We'll be in touch, Mrs Woods.'

'You need to lock him up,' Wendy said. 'Pervert.'

Bob and April left the room and walked down the corridor. Bob whistled a tune she didn't recognise.

'That went well,' she said sarcastically. 'Well played there, Bob.'

'I thought so,' Bob said, nodding.

'I was being sarcastic.'

'Really?'

'Yes.'

'So was I,' Bob said. 'Rio Woods is a liar. I just needed to be sure before we speak to Metcalfe.'

'We need to arrest him and interview him at the station just to cover our backsides.'

'I disagree. This has got 'no further action' written all over it,' Bob said.

'The boy has a broken nose, three stitches in the back of his head, and bruised genitals,' April said.

'And three witnesses saw him stumbling about in the Dingle,' Bob argued. 'He fell on his face and banged the back of his head. None of the witnesses saw him before he went into the water. This is NFA or my name isn't Robert.'

'We'll be arresting him.'

'Have it your way. We'll be arresting him, he'll be charged and released, and the CPS will NFA it. If this goes to court, it will fall at the first fence,' Bob said.

'Because of what, exactly?'

'Rio's lying,' Bob said. 'I saw the way he looked at you when we walked in.'

'What are you talking about?'

'He's a fifteen-year-old walking-erection and I think he's far from the innocent victim in this. Metcalfe assaulted him for a reason, and I'm guessing it's something to do with his daughter,' Bob said. 'I'll put money on it. And if it is to do with a sexual approach on a thirteen-year-old girl, the CPS will drop it like it's a big stinky turd.'

CHAPTER 9

Pamela Stone and her team made an initial sweep of the house. She could feel Kim everywhere. Her perfume tainted the air along with the fabric conditioner and scented candles she used. Beneath those pleasant fragrances were the unwholesome odours of the crimes committed in her home. The smell of spent shotgun cartridges, blood, and bleach lingered on the senses. They didn't belong in this home.

Pamela felt anxious. Kim had become more than a colleague over the years and they'd become close. It was hard to talk about work with people not in the job, not because of confidentiality but because civies didn't get it. There were many nights they drank wine and chatted until the sun came up, and they could no longer think straight. Sharing their thoughts and baring their souls was cathartic. It was a blessed release from the stresses and strains of the careers they'd chosen and the men they loved. The fact she was missing made her both very sad and very angry. Someone had targeted Kim for whatever reason, and they meant to harm or kill her. The booby trap left for whoever came to look for her was designed to kill them. The perpetrator wasn't fooling around. That was clear.

Pamela studied the frame the shotgun had been attached to. It wasn't bespoke, it was an ingenious adaptation of an everyday item. Manufactured in the millions to encase petrol generators used by campers and outdoor traders. The gun was common enough, and any traceable markings had been filed off. Kim's bedding had been removed, but there were bloodstains on the mattress and an attempt to clean them had failed. The mattress was wet in patches. She looked under the bed. It was thick with dust and hair, which she would expect to find in the bedroom of anyone who worked the hours a senior detective did. Her home was clean, but not sterile and detailed. The intruder, or intruders, hadn't left anything obvious to work with.

One of her team was working on the drawers and their contents. Pamela left the bedroom and went downstairs, checking each room was being processed. The work was being done in silence. The atmosphere sombre. Rob was in the kitchen.

'How are we getting on?' Pamela asked.

'Her bedding and five towels are in the washing machine,' Rob said. He was sorting the damp items onto a plastic sheet on the floor. It covered most of the kitchen tiles. 'Kim didn't put them on to wash. Whoever put them in there put laundry capsules in the wrong drawer and set them on a cold wash, so the bloodstains are still there.' Pamela inspected the washing. The bedsheets and pillows were heavily stained. The bloodstains were pink and faded, but they were still visible. 'It looks to me like the towels were used to clean up. The stair carpet has several wet patches, and the landing has two. Luminol is showing blood splatter. Lots of it.'

'Let's get it to the lab asap and establish if it's Kim's. If it is, we have to assume she's dead or at least critically injured. No one can lose that much blood.'

'Did she have any animals?' Rob asked. 'A large dog, maybe?'

Pamela shook her head. Tears filled her eyes.

'No. The blood is human. Kim's or someone else's.'

'If it's Kim's, why clean it up?' Rob asked. 'Makes me think it belongs to an intruder with forensic knowledge.'

'Maybe. Or it could be to make sure whoever came upstairs didn't stop in their tracks,' Pamela said. 'If the stairs were caked in blood, Alan may have been more cautious and waited for back-up and forensics before opening the bedroom door. He thought she was alive in her bedroom. That's why he dropped his guard.' She paused and wiped a tear from the corner of her eye.

'I know you were tight.' He tactfully changed the subject. 'Is there anything interesting in the bedroom?'

'The gun's been adapted. Both barrels were shortened to spread the blast enough to hit anyone standing in the doorway. It's a precise adaptation, measured and trialled. None of the pellets hit the walls either side of the door. That's not an accident. They didn't want to waste any shot by sawing the barrels off completely.' She shrugged. 'The stand is a tubular frame, probably from a portable generator. The type that's started with a pull cord. It was fixed to the frame with a couple of clamps and some solder. When it fired, it kicked itself against the wall, but the aim was true. There are no prints on it.' She shrugged.

'How did they set it ready to fire from the landing?'

'There's a pulley and a weight behind the door,' Pamela explained. 'They set it up, closed the door, and the weight caused the tension on the line.' She frowned. 'There was no way to open that door without setting off the shotgun.'

'I've seen something similar online,' Rob said. 'It would be easy to find the instructions on how to build it.'

'Are there any signs of a break in?'

'No. All the door locks and windows are secure.'

'Have we checked her car yet?'

'No. Shall we do it together?'

'Alan used a spare key to get in, right?' Jo said.

'Yes. He had a spare.'

They walked across the kitchen to the adjoining door. It was open. 'Maybe she entered the house through this door.'

'The garage door is an up and over and it's automatic,' Rob said, checking the motor. 'She could open it as she approached the house by remote and when she was inside, it would have closed itself. No need to use the front door.' He tried the passenger door, and it opened. 'The car's open.'

'There's blood on the floor,' Pamela said, pointing to an evidence marker. She was between the driver's door and the kitchen. 'There was a struggle here. There's blood on the car door, the floor, the wall, and ceiling. Check under the car, Rob,' she said.

'No problem, boss,' Rob said as he dropped to his knees. He pressed his face to the ground and looked beneath the vehicle. 'There's a tool under here,' he said. 'It looks like a hand axe.'

'How did they miss that on the first pass?'

'It's behind the front tyre,' Rob said. 'If they looked under here from the other side, it wouldn't be visible.'

'Let's get a picture of it in situ and then let's get it out of there,' Pamela said. 'Brian,' she called into the kitchen. The photographer poked his head around the door.

'Hello,' he said cheerily. Too cheerily.

'Rob's found a tool under the car. Can you get a few shots of it please?'

'No problem,' Brian said. He took pictures of it from the front and the side of the vehicle. 'You can crack on now.'

'Thanks.'

'Anything else in here?' he asked.

'Not for now, thanks.'

Rob reached under the vehicle with a grabber. He retrieved the tool and held it up so they could get a good look at it.

'Look here,' Rob said. There was debris on it. 'This is skin and hair and blood on the blade and this hair doesn't belong to Kim. It's the wrong colour.'

'Someone was hit over the head with it,' Pamela agreed. 'It explains the splatter in here.'

'If there was a struggle here, who hit who?' Rob said. 'I noticed a pile of logs next to the garden wall. I think the axe belongs to Kim.'

'I agree. There's a log burning stove in the dining room,' Pamela said. 'That would explain the axe being here.'

'This isn't Kim's hair, which means it belongs to her attacker.'

'She may have fought back.'

'If she picked up this, she put up a hell of a fight. We need to get this to the lab and tested yesterday,' he said, excited. 'If the attacker's in the system, we're halfway there.'

'Bag it and take samples of the blood and hair and take it back to the lab yourself. I'll get Richard to get you a police escort,' Pamela said, nodding. 'With an interceptor clearing the traffic, you could be there in just over an hour. It's the fastest way. That DNA could tell us who has Kim.'

Chapter 10

April and Bob arrived at the Metcalfe home in Trearddur Bay. Following the death of his wife three years prior, Ernie had put the family home up for sale and bought a six-bedroom house on Lon Isallt. The front of the house overlooked Craig-y-Mor, the iconic 'spooky house' perched on an outcrop next to the sea. His mother and father sold their home too and moved into a bungalow next door. The rear looked up at the old Cliff Hotel, which had been turned into holiday flats decades ago. At first, it was the ideal setup. His mother, Rose, helped with the girls when needed and when she wasn't required, his parents had their own space with a stunning view of the sea and the mountains and the Llyn Peninsula all the way to Bardsey Island. They only had to cross the road to be at the sea and the pebble beach and the girls absolutely loved it.

Losing their mother had been hard for them, and there were times when Ernie felt he couldn't cope with their grief as well as his own. His daughters seemed to pass the grief around like a relay team passing on the baton. No sooner had he settled one of them, another broke down. He had to explain to them that missing their mother was okay and that not being okay was okay too. Their tears were the most natural thing and they would miss her as long as they lived, although the pain would ease with time. He kept his own grief within the cauldron of anger, which permanently bubbled inside him. Keeping a lid on it was a constant battle.

His mother had been a rock despite his father's failing health and a short, one-sided battle with prostate cancer. It was six weeks from diagnosis to death. The cancer had spread through his body, attacking his critical organs and bones and it was too far gone to treat with chemo or radiation. His death had added to the family's glue, and they dealt with their grief as a unit as well as a family can.

Ernie was the best father he could be, considering he was a murdering psychopath. He struggled with his mental health but appeared to be a well-balanced individual on the surface. Sometimes, guilt crippled him, other times, he couldn't care less. Striking the balance between acceptable and unacceptable behaviour in his mind was a constant challenge. His temper was short and violent, but he kept it under control around his family. No one knew of the turmoil in his soul. He functioned well, but below the surface was mayhem. His mental issues were hidden behind a cleverly crafted facade.

Despite his demons, the girls didn't want for anything. They were doing well at school and they were polite and well behaved. Everyone said they were a credit to him and his dearly departed wife. Their existence was as normal as the next family's and they were financially well off. The arrival of Rio Woods on the scene was uninvited and most unwelcome. It had rocked the boat and prodded a troubled mind.

'Nice spot,' Bob said, looking at the house. 'Shall we see if Mr Metcalfe is agreeable to having a chat here before we decide if we're going to drag him down to the station and kick his teeth in?'

'We don't do that anymore,' April said.

'Really?' Bob said, shaking his head. 'I must have missed that email.'

'On any other day, he would already be in the cells interviewed by detectives.' April looked across the bay and watched the waves lapping on the rocks at Porth Diana. 'We've caught the short straw here.'

'I don't think he's being arrested with what we have. Not initially,' Bob argued. 'Not every time. There's more to this than meets the eye.'

'I think we should arrest him and speak to him formally,' April said. 'The assault is undeniable.'

'That's where you're wrong,' Bob said.

'I don't follow.'

'If he denies it, we have bugger all. Let's see what his reaction is. We can interview him in his home under caution,' Bob said. 'The station will be a circus for the next few days. What's the difference?'

'Rio Woods has considerable injuries. That's the difference.'

'Injuries which could be explained by his falling in the Dingle.'

'I know what you think, but the facts can't be ignored. He's a minor and the sexual element leaves us wide open to the press making a meal of it and his parents suing us.'

'It's not sexual.'

'You don't know that.'

'I do. Metcalfe grabbed him by the goolies as a warning,' Bob said. 'Not as foreplay.'

'Goolies?' April said, nodding. She giggled and shook her head. 'That takes me back to basic training. Our self-defence instructor used to say, "punch them in the throat or kick them in the goolies and you can't go wrong".' She shrugged. 'There wasn't much variation on that. He was ancient like you.'

'I'm experienced, not ancient.'

'I think he said that, too. What he failed to tell us was what to do if we missed their goolies or worse, if we hit the target but didn't disable them.' April looked at Bob. Her face became serious again. 'I don't think we can say grabbing a fifteen-year-old boy, who is a minor' – she reinforced the word – 'by the goolies to the point where he has severe bruising to his penis and testicles, head-butting him, smashing his skull against a tree trunk, and tossing him into a fast-moving stream was a warning.'

'Are you saying that's his idea of chatting him up for sex?'

'Of course not.'

'It's a warning. One-hundred per cent.'

'Whatever his motive, it was a viscous, violent assault, no matter what the reason.' She shook her head. 'I may be more sympathetic to the boy because I'm a mother of young children but it does beg the question of what the fuck are you thinking?'

'I take it you don't agree with me?' Bob asked sarcastically. April opened her mouth and then closed it without speaking. 'There are two sides to every story and we've only heard one. Let's remain impartial and ask him what his side is, yes?'

'Okay,' April said. 'Then we arrest him for assault.'

'Regardless of what he says?'

'Regardless of what his excuse is,' April said.

'Then we kick his teeth in?' Bob asked. April rolled her eyes. 'Oh, yes. Sorry. We don't do that anymore.'

CHAPTER 11

ACC Bill Armstrong arrived at headquarters in St Asaph. The chief constable was in her office and he noticed the subdued atmosphere in the station as he walked through the maze of corridors. The attack on their colleagues had hit the force's morale hard. It made each officer contemplate their own mortality and realise how fragile their grip on this existence really was. Every time they left home and said goodbye to their loved ones could be the last. Nothing is guaranteed. Bill could sense the mood in the building was subdued. When he finally reached her suite, he waved hello to the chief's receptionist.

'How are you?' he asked.

'I'm good thank you,' the receptionist answered. He didn't know her name, as she was new. 'Terrible news from the island.'

'Yes. It is.'

'Is there any news on Chief Inspector Williams?'

'None as yet,' Bill said. 'Is the chief alone?'

'Yes. She's held all her calls and is waiting for you.'

'Best not to keep her waiting then,' he said, knocking on the door.

'Can I get you a drink?'

'Coffee please. Black, no sugar, thank you.' He heard the chief calling him and opened the door. Diane Warburton was sitting behind her oak desk. She was an attractive woman with the physique of a ballet dancer. Her eyes were bright and full of intelligence. 'Are you free?' Bill asked.

'Yes. Come in,' Diane said. 'Take a seat. How are things at DI Davies' house?'

'It was chaos but it's organised finally,' Bill said. 'We've drafted in Gareth Jones from Caernarfon and Alison Walsh from St Asaph as SIOs for now.'

'They're both excellent DIs,' Diane said. 'They'll steady the ship.'

'The CSI team are still processing it. Pamela Stone called me with an update as I arrived here.'

'That sounds encouraging.'

'Yes. She had good news. They've found blood in the garage and an axe with DNA on it,' he explained. 'It was underneath Kim's car behind a tyre so it was missed on the first pass.'

'An axe?' Diane said, frowning. 'That doesn't sound like good news for Kim Davies.'

'They found hair and skin on the blade,' he said. 'The hair isn't Kim's, so we can assume it belongs to her attacker.' Diane nodded in agreement. 'It looks like she may have been attacked when she got out of her car and she defended herself. They've taken the weapon back to the lab on the Wirral with an interceptor escort. It should take just over an hour. They're going to rush the DNA and hope for a match.' Diane listened, her fingers steepled beneath her chin. 'We could get lucky if they're in the system.'

'Stranger things have happened,' Diane said. 'I'm conscious that your best detective is in surgery and his partner is missing. Have you thought about who to make Senior Investigating Officer?'

'If they have to be from another force, I want Detective Superintendent Olivia Mann from GMP. I worked with her many times when I was in the gang unit. She's the sharpest detective I've seen in many years.'

'I've heard good things about her,' Diane said. 'Second choice would be?'

'Ideally backed up by DI Jo Jones from Merseyside. She's in the Matrix Unit.'

'I know of her. You're in the realms of fantasy league with those two,' Diane said. She sighed and nodded. 'I might be able to play the 'It's two of our own who have been attacked' card,' she said. 'They would be the dream team, but don't hold your breath. We may only come up with the B-team. Let me see what I can do.'

'Thank you.'

'Don't thank me yet,' Diane said. 'We need an SIO on this today, and those two detectives are the cream of the crop. They'll be working on complex cases. They may need a week or so to hand over their caseload, and we don't have a week. I'll get you every spare detective we have, but you're going to have to babysit the investigation for now.'

'I'm more than happy to run with it,' Bill said. 'I'm going to set up my office in Holyhead as soon as we're done here.'

'Have you come all the way here to tell me that you're basing yourself on the island?' Diane said, eyeing him suspiciously. Bill shuffled uncomfortably in his seat. 'If that's why you're here, we could have done this on the phone,' Diane said.

'I wanted to speak to you about one aspect of the case face to face,' Bill said. 'I didn't want to discuss it on the telephone.'

'That sounds ominous.'

'Just a little delicate and best aired before the investigation picks up speed.' Bill cleared his throat.

'Come on, spit it out,' Diane said, frowning.

'It seems to be common knowledge there was an ongoing relationship between Alan Williams and Kim Davies.' Diane nodded almost imperceptibly but didn't speak. 'No one at the scene was surprised that he entered her home with a spare key.' Bill waited for a response but none came. 'They are in a personal, sexual relationship…'

'Yes. I believe so.' Diane shuffled some papers and looked uncomfortable. 'They've worked together for years. I'm not sure it's relevant to the investigation.'

'I wanted to clarify it from the start.'

'Where are you going with this?' Diane said.

'Their relationship clearly isn't news to you?'

'I'm aware of their situation and it's complex. They're more long-term friends than partners. Although they were serious in the distant past, it didn't work out. I'm informed they're both committed to living alone, so it's no concern of mine if they share a bed occasionally,' Diane said. 'There has never been even a hint of an issue at work and they make a very effective team. Somethings are best left untouched if possible.' Diane waited for a reaction. Bill looked pensive. 'Are you reading too much into this?'

'Maybe.' Bill shrugged. 'My thought process is that whoever left the booby trap in the bedroom knew the first person to walk through it would most likely be a keyholder?'

'Not necessarily but carry on.'

'I'm thinking what the most likely sequence of events would be from the attacker's point of view.'

'And?'

'Kim's absence from work would be noted and they would try to contact her,' Bill said. 'Eventually, they would go to her home and force entry unless someone there had a key.'

'Which Alan did.'

'Assuming the attackers knew that, they intended to kill DCI Williams when he came looking for her by rigging up a booby trap.'

'It's likely they meant to kill or seriously injure whoever responded first, but how could they know it would be Alan?'

'I'm exploring motives and the woman he's been in a long-term relationship with is missing, so I would like to eliminate her from the list of suspects.'

'Do you have a list of suspects yet?' Diane asked, frowning.

'No but you get my meaning,' Bill said, shrugging.

'You're not suggesting she staged an attack at her home in order to blast Alan with a shotgun?'

'Of course, not,' Bill said. 'That sounds ridiculous.'

'It does.'

'Could there be anyone else on the periphery of their relationship?' Bill asked, shrugging.

'Such as?'

'A jealous third party with an axe to grind. Pardon the pun.' Bill sighed and sat forward in his chair. 'This appears to be personal to me. It doesn't feel like a hammer-blow at the authorities. I'm asking if there's been anyone affected by their relationship?'

'I doubt it.' Diane ran her fingers through her hair, thoughtfully. 'You need to tread very carefully if you intend to explore that avenue,' Diane said. 'Alan and his team are fiercely loyal to one another. That's one of the reasons they're so effective. Keep your ear to the ground in the Holyhead station, but don't actively seek any dirt on either of them,' she stressed. 'Station gossip will spill out to the press and the public very quickly, and I don't want rumours and speculation clouding the issue. I want everyone onside with this investigation. Are we clear?'

'Crystal,' Bill said, standing up. Her expression told him the conversation was over. 'I'll get myself back to the island immediately.'

'Good,' Diane said. 'Call me once you're settled with an update.'

Chapter 12

Ernie Metcalfe opened the door and looked surprised to see uniformed police officers standing there. He was wearing joggers, a fleece hoodie, and a pair of slippers. The wind was blowing off the sea, cold and salty, and moody clouds scampered across the sky towards Snowdonia. He recognised Bob Dewhurst as the local bobby. Trearddur Bay was a huge tourist Mecca, but when all the visitors went home, it was essentially just a small coastal village where everyone knew everyone. They had crossed paths when he was RAF police at Valley but had never spoken.

'Hello,' Ernie said, lifting his spectacles from his face. 'Excuse me, I was reading the newspaper. Can I help?'

'Good afternoon, Mr Metcalfe,' April said. 'I'm Sergeant Byfelt and this is Sergeant Dewhurst.' The two men nodded silently at each other. 'We're investigating an assault which took place earlier today at Menai Bridge.' Ernie looked confused. 'We need to ask you some questions.'

'You need to ask me questions about an assault which took place in Menai Bridge?'

'Yes.'

'What do you need to ask me about an assault in Menai Bridge?' Ernie asked, frowning. 'Are you at the right house?'

'It might be better if we come inside and talk about it?' April said.

'I'm on my way out,' Ernie said, shaking his head. 'I have an appointment at the doctors and as you can see, I'm not dressed yet.' He looked from one officer to the other and shrugged. 'If you need to ask me any questions, do it here and make it quick.'

'This is a very serious matter,' April said.

'I'm sure it is or you wouldn't be here,' Ernie said, half smiling. His eyes narrowed slightly and became piercing. 'I don't know anything about an assault in Menai Bridge and you're not coming in without a warrant, so get on with it. What do you need to ask me?'

'Where were you at eight fifty-five this morning?' April asked.

'That's a simple one to answer. I was in bed,' Ernie said.

'In bed?' April asked, shaking her head. 'Was there anyone in the house who can confirm that?'

'Yes. Everyone who lives here can confirm it. My mother and three daughters,' Ernie said. 'I've been struggling with a bad back, hence my appointment with the doctor. Mum got the girls ready this morning, and they left here about nine-ish.' April and Bob listened, uneasy with his explanation. Ernie could see the doubt in their eyes. 'They all go to school in Bodedern and they start at nine-thirty. I was in bed when they left here. They all said goodbye before they left.' He paused. 'Does that answer your question?'

'You weren't in Menai Bridge?' April asked.

'Are you deaf or are you calling me a liar?'

'Just answer the question,' Bob said. 'You know the score, Mr Metcalfe. We have a job to do. A crime has been committed and we have to investigate.'

'Okay. Sorry. No. I wasn't in Menai Bridge this morning. I was here,' Ernie said, sighing. His eyes were dark and marbled. They didn't give anything away. He shrugged. 'I can see you don't believe me, so let's put this to bed, shall we? Mum!' he shouted down the hallway. Rose appeared from a room to their left, carrying a newspaper. 'Can you come here a minute, please?'

'Yes. What's the matter?' she asked, approaching the door.

'This is my mother, Rose,' Ernie said.

Rose approached and saw the uniforms, and she looked concerned. 'Hello,' she said. 'Why are the police here? Is anything wrong?'

'It's nothing to be worried about. I think there's been a misunderstanding, but we're here to verify where Ernie was this morning,' Bob said, seeing an opportunity. 'At about nine-ish?'

'He was here in bed,' Rose said without hesitation. 'I took the girls to school this morning as his back's been playing up, hasn't it, dear?'

'Yes, it has,' Ernie said. 'I've explained that to the officer already, but they need it confirming.'

'What time did you leave here?' April asked.

'About nine o'clock.'

'And you spoke to Ernie before you left?'

'Yes. What's this about?'

'That's great,' April said, ignoring the question. 'We're sorry to have bothered you. There must have been a mistake in the information we received.'

'No problem,' Ernie said. 'It happens. I was RAF police myself, stationed at Valley, so I know how unreliable witnesses can be.'

'We know who you are,' Bob said. 'Sorry to bother you.'

'Not a problem. Still, you have a job to do and I have an appointment to keep, so if you don't mind...' Ernie said, stepping back from the door. He was about to close it.

'Do you know a teenager by the name of Rio Woods?' Bob asked.

'Doesn't ring a bell,' Ernie said, straight-faced. His eyes met Bob's, and they held his gaze. Not a flicker. 'Rio Woods. No. Should I know him?'

'He's a friend of your daughter, Helen,' Bob said. Ernie didn't flinch. His face was deadpan. Not even a flicker in his eyes.

'No. Sorry,' Ernie said. 'I've never heard of him. If you don't mind,' he said, looking at his watch. 'I need to be somewhere...'

'Of course, you do,' Bob said. 'We'll be on our way. Sorry to have bothered you, Mr Metcalfe.'

The front door closed, and the officers walked back to their vehicle. Waves splashed against the seawall across the road, the sound soothing and familiar. Bob climbed in and opened his window. April followed suit.

'Now what?' April said.

A Disturbing Thing Happened Today

'This is a dead end but either Rio Woods ran into a tree and then jumped into the Dingle to frame Ernest Metcalfe for assaulting him, or that man is a very accomplished liar, either way, we have a suspect with a cast-iron alibi. Four alibis, in fact.'

'You believe Woods has identified the right man?' April asked.

'Yes,' Bob said, nodding. 'And I'm sure Metcalfe assaulted the boy because of his daughter, but it doesn't matter what I think. Something has happened between those teenagers, and Metcalfe has overreacted.'

'I wasn't expecting him to say he was at home all morning,' April said, sighing.

'I thought he was going to say he confronted Woods, and it got out of hand.' Bob agreed. 'The fact he's denying being there at all has thrown me completely.'

'Someone's lying.'

'You should be a detective.'

'Fuck off, Bob,' April said, frowning. 'He's done my head in. I don't need you joining in. What about the other three witnesses?' April said.

'You mean his daughters? It's worth asking them if they saw their father this morning,' Bob said. 'I didn't get the impression his mother was lying, did you?'

'No,' April said, shaking her head. 'But he can't be in two places at once. We can ask if we have enough to get a warrant for the GPS on his phone. In the meantime, let's go and speak to the head teacher at Bodedern. We can't speak to the girls, but we might be able to twist her arm to ask them if they saw their father this morning.'

CHAPTER 13

Kim woke up with a start. At first, her mind was blank. Then memories of the attack flooded back to her like a tsunami of fear. She remembered being at home, drinking a glass of wine, when she heard a noise from beyond the kitchen. She'd gone to investigate, and the garage door was in the process of closing. Someone had opened it. She remembered stepping into the garage and approaching the driver's side. The door being opened and the cold air rushing in from outside. A rubber Halloween clown mask. Pennywise or the Joker, she wasn't sure which. The driver's door flying open. The pig's head mask, which was even more frightening than the fucking clown mask. A blow to the head, which sent her spinning. Another punch from the side, this time to her jaw. Her senses were reeling. She felt a hand grabbing her hair and yanking her head back sharply, stopping her from moving. A punch to the mouth from the pig mask man split her lips and white lightning flashed in her brain. Then she felt a sharp prick in her neck. A syringe. They had injected her with something…

Despite the confusion and pain, she realised she'd been blitzed by at least three attackers but none of them spoke a word. The memories blurred at the point she had passed out, but she had snippets of being moved in pitch-darkness. No one had spoken a word throughout the attack, not even to each other. The attackers had planned their assault with skill and professionalism. Their timing and precision were to be feared and admired. That was a bad thing; outfits with this level of skill were frighteningly dangerous and could make a person disappear in a matter of minutes. She was in deep trouble, and she knew it. Ice-cold fear flowed through her veins. A dozen questions flowed through her mind. Why had they attacked her? What did they want? Where was she now and what were they planning to do with her?

She opened her eyes, but it made no difference to the complete darkness that she found herself in. She blinked but could see nothing but tiny dust swirls moving against an inky blackness. Was she blind, or was she in a room with no light seeping in? Maybe she was in a vehicle, or maybe she was underground. Her brain processed what her senses were telling her. She focused and could feel bindings around her head and face. That was why it was so dark. It had to be. She was in a dreadful situation; she knew that much.

She tried to sit up, but she was restrained. Her muscles ached and cramped, and she tried to move her arms, but they were bound together at the wrists and also fastened to her abdomen with metal bracelets. She could hear the metal chink. Handcuffs or shackles of some kind. She tried to kick her legs, but they were fastened at the ankles, her feet wide apart. Her inner thigh muscles burnt and tingled, complaining at the unnatural stretch, and her hips ached. A cold draft touched her skin, and she realised she was only partially dressed. She was blindfolded, restrained, and extremely vulnerable. She panicked and thrashed around, trying to escape the bonds and the darkness, but she was pinned in position like a butterfly to a board awaiting dissection. She felt like her heart was going to explode. Her breathing was coming in short burning gasps and her lungs felt constricted. She was being suffocated by her own terror. It was all she could do to try to slow her breathing. She couldn't allow panic to take control of her senses, and she tried to focus on her breathing. Deep breath in, slowly blow it out, deep breath in, blow it out and repeat.

A door opened to her right, and she froze in fear. Cold air rushed in, tickling her skin, giving her goosebumps. She heard a light switch being flicked, but couldn't see the light. Footsteps approached her.

'I heard you thrashing around. You're awake, are you?' a male voice said. It was deep, and the accent wasn't local to the island. Not Anglesey at least. He was Irish. Probably from the north. 'You must be wondering where you are and why you're here?'

Kim listened but tried not to move. She felt helpless. She sensed the man step closer. His presence was malevolent. She sensed danger like never before.

'I think the not knowing must be driving you mad,' he said. 'You must be wondering what's going to happen to you.' Kim remained quiet. He squeezed her thigh above the knee, and she recoiled at his touch. His hand moved higher. 'You have good thighs. If it was up to me, I'd keep you here for a while and fuck you until I got bored or you starved to death, whichever came first.' She sensed evil in his tone. He moved closer. She felt his hand on her other thigh and she twisted and writhed but couldn't move more than a few inches. His touch on her bare skin gave her goosebumps and made her feel nauseous.

'Get your fucking hands off me!' she shouted.

'Ah, she speaks,' he said. 'And you have a potty mouth too.'

'You've heard nothing yet,' Kim snapped.

'A fighter, eh?' The man squeezed her flesh. 'I like that.'

'Get your hands off me!'

'I don't think so.'

'Who are you?' she shouted. 'What do you want?'

'I can't tell you that.'

'Why am I here?' Kim asked, losing control.

'That's an easy one. Because you're a pig and you've been snuffling around with your big pig nose, sticking it in people's business. People who don't appreciate their business being fucked around with,' he said. 'You know what happens to pigs, don't you?' he said, pinching the skin on her inner thigh between his finger and thumb. He twisted it hard. She cried out and bit her lip against the pain. 'Pigs get sliced up and roasted and others get minced and turned into sausages.' He chuckled. She felt his face near hers, his breath through the material. He smelt of cigarettes and weed. It made her feel physically nauseous. 'Would you rather be a chop or a sausage?'

'Fuck you!'

'You will do, if I get my way. But you won't enjoy it. Not for one minute.'

'Please tell me what I'm doing here?'

'Do you like being handcuffed?' he whispered, moving his hand up her thigh. 'You must feel very vulnerable. Are you frightened?'

'Fuck off,' Kim said, thrashing about, but she could hardly move an inch.

'It's not much fun being cuffed, is it?'

His hand went further up her inner thigh. Kim froze, desperately trying to close her legs. She felt hot tears running down her cheeks.

'Get off me!'

'I haven't even got going yet,' he whispered in her ear.

'What the fuck are you doing?' another voice growled. 'Get your grubby little hands off her.'

'Ooh, grubby hands, indeed,' the first man said sarcastically. 'The fun police are here. Looks like we'll have to wait until another time,' he whispered to her.

'Get away from her.'

'What are you getting so worked up about?' the first man asked, walking away. 'She your little sister or something?'

'I warned you there would be none of your weird shit this time,' the other man said. His accent was from the south of Ireland; much softer.

'Weird shit?' the man repeated. 'Don't you like women?'

'Get out of here, you freak. You make me sick.'

'That's because you're weak. You're a pussy. If it wasn't for your brother, I'd bash your brains out and feed you to the fish.' He chuckled. It was an evil sound. 'I might do it anyway.'

'I don't need my brother to fight my battles and when this is done, if you want to test your mettle, I'm more than happy to help. In fact, I'll look forward to it,' he said. 'Now get out of here and go and fetch the supplies from the van.'

'Are you gay?' the first man asked, his tone sarcastic. 'She's a good-looking woman, and she's tied up. I see an opportunity there as a red-blooded male, but clearly you don't. Do you prefer men?'

'Get out and get the gear from the van.'

'Are you a friend of Gloria?'

'I won't tell you again.'

'It's a fair question,' the man pushed. 'Do you prefer a penis to a vagina?' There was no reply. 'I reckon you're a sword swallower, aren't you?'

She heard a metallic click. The men were silent for long seconds.

'That's a nice blade,' the first man said. 'I hope you know how to use it because if you don't, I'll take it off you and shove it through your neck.'

'Why don't you give that a try to let's see how it works out for you?'

There was complete silence. All she could hear was her blood pumping through her ears. She held her breath and prayed that the second man would stab the first through the heart, so that he couldn't put his hands on her again. Or worse.

'Okay. You win, gay boy,' the first man said, sarcastically. 'Watch your back from now on. You've got the blade this time. Next time we'll be evenly matched.'

'Get out. I've heard enough of your shit.'

Kim heard the first man leave the room. There was quiet for a moment, then she heard the light switch being flicked, the door closed and locked. She breathed a sigh of relief, but she knew it was a temporary reprieve.

Chapter 14

Belinda Preece listened to the summing up from the defence barrister. It was probably the biggest pile of shite ever compiled into a mitigating circumstances case that she'd ever had to listen to. Consideration of the argument would be swift and brutal, her mind already made up. She would influence the jury as much as she could in summing up without actually telling them to find the defendant guilty. The accused was a scumbag with a record as thick as the hardback version of War and Peace. If ever there had been a guiltier man in her courtroom, she couldn't remember one. He had shaken his stepdaughter to death and tried to cover it up, first by placing her body in her cot and making it look as if she was sleeping and denying any knowledge, second by blaming her mother, who was classed as a vulnerable adult with learning difficulties and a mental health diagnosis. It had been a difficult case to listen to without adding the distress caused to the child's mother, which was significant. The accusations had to be investigated, which had further traumatised the young woman. She was overwhelmed with grief. Her suffering was visible to everyone in the courtroom and the distress caused by the cross-examination was unbearable to watch. The medical evidence proved conclusively the circle of guilt had been explored and the mother was working when the child had been killed. The timeline was undeniable, and the accused was the only possible perpetrator. He was a child killer and lying bastard and she was going to send him away for as long as she possibly could with as much impartiality as she could muster.

Despite the defence barrister's objections, Judge Preece had cut the cross-examination short to save the mother from any further torment. His summing up consisted of blaming his client's behaviour on his upbringing and a lifelong addiction to alcohol and drugs. His upbringing had been challenging, but there was nothing presented in evidence to point to him being damaged by it. Basically, nothing was his fault, but the truth was the predicament he found himself in was because he was a cunt. It was a pity she couldn't actually say that to the accused and his barrister, but decorum was king in the courtroom. When the defence rested, she adjourned the hearing while the jury considered their verdict. It was Friday afternoon and pointless returning before Monday, which suited her down to the ground. She wanted to share a few bottles of chardonnay with friends in the Black Boy, Caernarfon's most famous pub.

She changed her blouse in her chambers and let down her hair, brushing it in the mirror. A dab of blusher and lipstick and a squirt of Armani and she was ready to begin the weekend. It had been a gruelling few weeks, and she needed to switch off. She called Melisa, her best friend, who was also a top local barrister. They met on the pavement near the castle wall and headed towards the pub. It was only a ten-minute walk. They chatted about their plans for the weekend and what they were going to eat later. Melisa always ordered the chef's special, whatever it was, and Belinda always had sea bass or sirloin. They did the same thing every second Friday without fail. Sometimes others joined them, but they were the constant attendees on their Friday night jaunts.

'How did it go with the baby killer?' Melisa asked. She lowered her voice. 'I didn't want to ask in the pub. There are too many big-eared nosey buggers in there.'

'The jury are out and I'm predicting a guilty verdict before lunchtime on Monday,' Belinda said. 'He's never going to see the light of day through an unbarred window for the rest of his days.'

'Good for you,' Melisa said. 'Bring back hanging. I'm happy to tie the knot.'

'Don't get me started,' Belinda said. 'Hey. Have you heard about Alan Williams from Holyhead?'

'Yes, but it's all Chinese whispers,' Melisa said. 'Kim Davies is missing, which is a real mystery. I mean, who kidnaps a detective inspector?'

'And shoots her boss?'

'Exactly. The world has gone fucking mental.'

'Totally fucked up.'

Belinda didn't hear the transit van approaching from behind them as they crossed High Street. Melisa did and turned to see what was coming just as the van mounted the pavement. She grabbed Belinda's arm and pulled her towards the wall, trying to get them out of the vehicle's path. The van accelerated as it neared and was doing fifty when it hit them. Both women were thrown a distance by the impact. Melisa landed in the road and was stunned. She tried to get up but was run over by the number eighty-eight bus to Llanberis, which couldn't stop in time. Belinda was thrown through the window of a card shop, her body half in and half out, legs twitching as if she was running in thin air. No one could describe the van driver as he sped away towards Bangor.

CHAPTER 15

Jimmy Woods was sitting in the Holland, drinking a pint of Guinness with two of his best friends, Wills and Conor. Wills came back from the bar with three double Jameson whiskeys. They called it a double-Irish round; Irish whiskey and Irish stout. Conor came back from the toilet and sat his considerable bulk down on a leather bar stool. He picked up his pint with a hand the size of a spade, his fingers like sausages. Wills gave them their whiskey. They clinked their glasses and emptied them in one swallow. The pub was quiet, and they kept their voices low as they spoke about what had happened.

'So, who is this fucking weirdo that attacked Rio?' Conor asked.

'A guy called Metcalfe. Rio said he's friends with his daughter on Facebook,' Jimmy said. 'He's never met the bloke before.'

'And the police said he's an ex-copper?' Wills asked.

'Yes. They said he has three daughters and is ex-services too.'

'So, he just attacked him without warning?' Wills asked.

'He was waiting along the path Rio takes to school. Rio said he stepped out from behind a tree and tried to grab his cock.'

'No way,' Conor said, shaking his head.

'Bad ye,' Wills added.

'Yes. Rio slapped him away, and he went nuts and butted him. The doctor said his knob is black and blue and his nose is broken.'

'That must hurt like fuck, ye,' Conor said. 'I can't believe this has happened. Then what did he do?'

Jimmy sipped his pint. 'Then he chucked him in the Dingle. He nearly drowned.'

'This guy is dangerous.'

'You're not wrong there,' Jimmy agreed.

'What are you going to do about it?' Conor asked. Jimmy looked confused. 'A paedo has grabbed your son's tackle and broke his nose. He needs to be punished, ye.'

'The courts will hammer him,' Jimmy said. 'He can't get away with that.'

'Courts?' Wills snorted. 'I don't think you should wait for the courts to deal with him, Jimmy.'

'What do you mean?' Jimmy asked.

'There's no way I would have some paedo attacking my son and not do something about it. What do you think, Conor?'

'The freak needs to be put in the ground, ye,' Conor said. 'He grabbed your son's cock and broke his nose. That's wrong in so many ways that I don't know where to begin.'

'I'm not sure what you're saying,' Jimmy said, aware others were listening now.

'You have to hurt this fucker, Jimmy.' Jimmy nodded and felt under pressure. He wasn't a violent man and couldn't fight to save his life. His friends were more akin to that side of things. Conor could find a fight in an empty room, but he weighed nearly twenty-stone and stood over six feet-four inches tall. He hadn't lost a fight since primary school. It was easy for him to say violence was the answer. Jimmy didn't have that gut instinct. 'You can't let him get away with that.' He lowered his voice and leant in closer. 'Once word gets around town that your son was attacked by a sexual predator, people will expect you to have done something about it, ye.' Jimmy nodded again but looked bemused. 'How was it left with the dibbles?'

'They were going to his house to interview him straight from the hospital, so I assume he'll be in the cells now,' Jimmy said. 'I don't know how these things work. What am I supposed to do?'

'They'll interview him, charge him, and release him,' Wills said. 'We need to be ready when he gets out of the station.'

'We?' Jimmy said, confused.

'Yes. We.' Conor patted him on the back. 'We're going to help you sort this fucker out, ye. We're not having a dirty paedo interfering with your Rio and getting away with it. He threw him in the stream and left him for dead. We could be sitting here arranging a funeral and deciding who's going to carry your boy's coffin, ye.' He held out his hand and Jimmy shook it, feeling small and weak in comparison to his big friend. 'Here's my hand, here's my heart. We're going to do this fucker and make sure he doesn't bother anyone's kids again.'

CHAPTER 16

Rio turned on his iPad and logged into the hospital Wi-Fi. He went into TikTok and Messenger and checked his conversations with Helen were deleted. They were all gone apart from one that was fairly bland, which was a relief. His text messages had been flirty at first and increasingly suggestive as time went by. He wondered if he had gone too far and crossed the line in respect of her age. Okay, she was a bit younger but she could pass for sixteen easily. No one could blame him for fancying her; she was well-fit. That said, his encounter with her father had rocked him to the core. What a fucking lunatic he was. He'd thrown him around like he was a rag doll. It had certainly made him stop and think about contacting her again. Not that it would stop him. If anything, he was more determined than ever to get her alone. There was no way that wanker was going to get away with what he'd done. Rio decided he was going to get a grip of Helen one way or another just to spite her crazy-fuck dad. The danger was intoxicating. He would have to be very discreet and avoid using his own profiles to message her on social media.

The memories of the attack echoed in his mind, and he had the pain and bruises to remind him. His eyes were black now and they would get worse before they got better. Helen would be horrified if she could see what her dad had done to him. Her dad had snatched his phone and read the messages they'd exchanged that morning and then taken his phone too. The message about kissing with her mouth open had sent him over the edge. That's what sent him into a rage even though Helen had said she wanted to learn how to snog properly. Mr Metcalfe had really lost his shit there and then. What a nutter. It was just snogging. What was his problem? Didn't everyone snog when they were young?

His mate, Cody, had explained how things worked. Kissing on the lips came first, then kissing with tongues, next was touching their tits over their jumper, then squeezing them underneath their jumper, and getting your hand inside their bra. Sucking their nipples was the ultimate top half activity and the gateway to trying to get into their knickers, fingering, which he called 'smelly finger' and so on and so on. Cody said, moving one step at a time was called chivalry, whatever that was. It all seemed very natural and made perfect sense, but Ernie Metcalfe had lost his shit about the kissing part, which was at the beginning. Fuck knows what he would do if they'd progressed further. Imagine if he'd said something about touching her downstairs and getting a smelly finger. His fucking head would have exploded.

Whatever he did next, he would have to be very careful. Metcalfe was fucking nuts and Rio had to be smarter than he was. He had to find a way to speak to her without arousing suspicion. If he told her what her dad had done to him, she might feel sorry for him and let him have a fumble as way of an apology. Cody told him about one girlfriend who gave him a 'sympathy wank' when his dog died, which doesn't sound outrageous until Cody said he never had a dog. He told this girl his dog died and feigned tears, so she hugged him and then one thing led to another. Rio could only aspire to be like Cody. He looked up to Cody as it was clear he was a ladies' man and knew what they wanted. What he didn't know about women wasn't worth knowing, and he was only sixteen.

Rio planned his strategy in his mind. His mum had reported his phone stolen and O2 had said they would send a replacement in the post the next day, but using his mobile to message her probably wasn't the best way to communicate. It was too easy to trace a message back to him. Ernie Metcalfe was a frightening man, and he didn't want to be confronted by him again, that was for sure. It would be better not to contact her at all, but he liked her. He really liked her. It would be okay as long as he could find a way to talk to her without him knowing. He wondered which messages he had seen before he contacted him on messenger to tell him to back off in the first instance. He thought her father was checking her phone somehow and reading her messages or how else could he have known? They weren't the type of messages a girl would show her dad voluntarily. There were plenty of piggy-back software apps around, some of them very cheap. He must have installed one of them in her mobile. How else could he have known they were talking?

That was spooky. He couldn't imagine his mum going through his phone, reading messages from his mates and checking what sites he was visiting. That would take some explaining and be the most embarrassing conversation ever. Cody said his mum restocked his condoms every Friday, ready for the weekend. How cool was she? Imagine having a mum so cool, she stocked up your condoms every Friday. Imagine having to need to stock up on condoms. Rio couldn't wait to be sixteen and have a box of condoms, although he would probably hide his and it would be a packet of three to begin with until he reached Cody's level. Rio couldn't think about talking to his mum about sex in any shape or form. She'd asked him if he'd been approached by Metcalfe in any way at all before the attack. Of course, he had said no, which was a lie, but what else could he say?

Actually, Mum, I've been chatting her up and her dad's found out. He told me to back off because she's thirteen and I told him to do one and take a chill-pill, then he read a text message I sent her offering to teach her how to kiss with her mouth open, that's probably why he twated me and threw me in the Dingle.

She would kick me all over Holyhead and back again, he thought. He checked for Helen's profiles. There was no sign of them. They'd been taken down, so had her Instagram account. It was an educated guess that her dad would also have blocked her mobile phone or taken it off her completely. Mr Metcalfe was battening down the hatches and sealing her off from social media and the outside world. He was obviously angry and trying to make sure she couldn't be contacted by Rio or anyone else.

Rio felt his nose throbbing and his testicles were aching. The painkillers were wearing off. Ernie Metcalfe had hurt him badly, and he wanted revenge. The man needed to be punished and if he was put in prison, Helen would be unprotected and fair game. Her dad was a fucking lunatic, but he wasn't going to stop Rio from seeing Helen. He would ask Cody for a few tips and find a way.

Chapter 17

Bob and April were sitting in the head teacher's office, explaining the situation to her. She wasn't happy with the intrusion or what they were asking her to do.

'I can't pull a child out of class and confront her with two police officers,' Betty Mills said. 'The poor girl would be terrified needless to say it would be illegal. Surely you know the rules?'

'We do,' April said. 'Of course, we do. We don't want to make a fuss and make the enquiries official. We don't feel that's helpful at this stage, so we wondered if you could ask her if she saw her father before she left for school this morning.' Betty Mills frowned. 'It's that simple. We just need to confirm he was at home when the girls left for school and then we'll be on our way.'

'What is this about?' the head asked.

'It's an ongoing enquiry so, we can't go into detail,' Bob said. 'We think it's something and nothing, but we have to establish a few facts before we can put it to bed.'

'Against my better judgement, I'll ask Helen if she saw her dad this morning before she left for school,' the head said, frowning again. 'I'll think of something to make it seem like an innocent question,' she added, standing. 'Please wait in here. Uniformed police officers wandering around school make everyone nervous.'

The head left the room, and they waited a few seconds to make sure she wasn't going to come back immediately. There was something about sitting in the head teacher's office that was unsettling. Scary memories from childhood, maybe.

'Did you hear that?' April asked.

'What?'

'You make people nervous.'

'I make Eileen nervous because she's never quite sure what I'm going to say next,' Bob said, nodding.

'Me and her both,' April said. 'I feel her pain.'

CHAPTER 18

Kim heard the door being unlocked and the light switch being flicked. Cold air touched her skin and fear coursed through her veins as she listened intently. Footsteps approached. At least two sets, she thought. She felt hands touching her bindings and the shackles being moved and twisted, then she heard a key being clicked in a lock.

'What's happening?' she asked, trying not to cry. She felt the handcuffs being removed from her wrists and the straps on her ankles were freed. The relief in her muscles was indescribable. Pins and needles spread through her limbs, numbing them and sending tingling sensations to her brain. 'Please tell me why I'm here?'

No one answered her question, but she was pulled up gently by the arms. Her head began to spin, the dizziness nauseating. Blood began to reach the extremities of her body again. She knew she'd been drugged and its effects were still lingering, clouding her senses. The pulse in her head thumped like a snare drum and it was difficult to swallow.

'Sit up straight but take it easy,' a voice said. It was the second man. The man with the knife who'd saved her from the pervert. That was a huge relief. 'Move slowly. You'll feel groggy and your limbs will be stiff but it will pass.'

'I need to use the toilet right now or things are going to get messy,' Kim said, her voice cracked. The face covering was claustrophobic and causing her immense distress. She felt like she was being smothered. 'And I need this fucking thing off my face. Please take it off me!'

'Okay. Calm down.'

'And I need a drink of water.'

'You'll get all those things in the next few minutes,' the voice said calmly. 'Spin your legs over the edge and stand up slowly.' Kim did as she was asked, trying not to become hysterical. She felt like she couldn't breathe, and she knew if she vomited, she'd choke to death. Her feet touched the floor. It was cold and hard, like concrete. Her toes were numb as she tried to put weight on her legs. The pain in her thighs was too much, and she buckled at the knee. 'Slowly,' the voice said. Strong hands held her upright. 'Stamp your feet, gently, and get the circulation going,' the man said. 'Hold your head still or you'll be sick.'

Kim felt a zip being unfastened at the back of her head. The facemask was removed, and she could see light through the material which covered her eyes. She blinked to help her eyes to adjust.

'I'm going to remove the blindfold now,' the man said. His voice was calm and soothing. 'The light will be bright at first and we're wearing Halloween masks, so don't be startled when you see them.

There's no need to be afraid at this point in time, although that may change, depending on your compliance.'

'Okay. Thank you,' Kim said, standing on shaky legs. The blindfold was removed, and she squinted against the lights and breathed deeply. Her hands went to her face instinctively. Being able to move was such bliss. A sports bottle was handed to her, and she gulped at it greedily. The water was cold and refreshing, soothing her throat as she drank. Her vision cleared, and she focused on the pig mask to her right. The man to her left was wearing the Pennywise mask. He was the man speaking. They were wearing boilersuits and gloves and wellington boots. There was nothing she could use to identify them. The room was bare brick in patches, the rest crumbling plaster. A single light bulb hung on a threadbare flex from a grimy ceiling, which hadn't been painted for decades. Cobwebs hung in each corner of the room, thick and coated with dust. It had the feel of a cellar or large farmhouse basement. The trolley she'd been lying on was from an ambulance or a hospital. It didn't belong there. She drank again and savoured the soothing liquid.

'What's going on? she asked. 'Why am I here?'

'You'll find out soon enough,' Pennywise said. He grabbed her elbow to support her weight. 'Put this on,' he said, handing her a dark boiler suit. 'I'm afraid we don't have anything in your exact size.'

'Where are my clothes?'

'You wet your jeans on the way here, so we removed them. It was a consequence of the tranquiliser we used. Please don't panic about your nudity, you have not been interfered with in any manner.' Kim blushed and took the suit. She clambered into it as quickly as she could, taking comfort in being covered up. 'We're going to see the boss and my advice is to answer the questions as honestly and in as much detail as you can.'

'I need the toilet,' she said, nodding. The men took her by the elbow and guided her through the door into a corridor, which was dark and dank. The floor was made from paving stones, worn smooth by decades of wear. One of the men opened a door, which was panelled wood, cracked by age. A porcelain toilet was fixed to the wall, a matching cistern above it. A rusty chain hung from the cistern and the sound of dripping water reached her. Gossamer webs hung in swathes from the walls. The toilet bowl was stained dark brown and stank of urine. She recoiled, but the urge to pee was overwhelming her. Kim closed the door and pulled the boilersuit down in the nick of time. The relief was indescribable. She closed her eyes and took a deep breath of the damp air, and it calmed her a little. Her senses were clearing slightly, and she tried hard to focus and get a grip of herself. She finished and redressed, pulling the boilersuit up and fastening it to the neck. The men were standing outside when she opened the door.

'Right,' she said. 'You said you want to ask me some questions?'

'The boss does.'

'Questions about what?' Kim asked, trying to make out the colour of his eyes beneath the mask. Light reflected from them. He was wearing shades beneath the mask. These guys left nothing to chance. They were professionals and well trained.

'Best you wait to hear it from the boss,' the man said. 'Please don't be under any illusion that because we've made you more comfortable, we're showing weakness,' he warned. 'It would be easier for us to torture the information from you and put you back into that room in the dark, lock the door and throw away the key. No one will be looking for you here and no one will stumble across you. You will be thirsty, starving, and afraid, and you will die alone in the dark. Am I making myself clear?'

'Perfectly clear,' Kim mumbled. She didn't want to be put back into the mask. It was the worst experience of her life, and she couldn't go back into the darkness of that room. The fear and dread had broken her and shattered her confidence. She felt weak and vulnerable and totally helpless. Whatever they wanted to know, she would tell them. There were no medals for being tortured, no matter how long you held out; everyone has a breaking point and suffering was beneficial to no one when the outcome was inevitable. She'd watched many films where the heroes don't divulge any information, regardless of the pain and suffering. Unfortunately, this was real life and unlikely to have a happy ending. They had broken her psychologically with the nature of the attack, its intensity, its professionalism, and the removal of her dignity. She had no other option available but to comply. 'Take me to him. I'll tell him whatever he needs to know.'

'Good. She'll be glad you want to cooperate,' the man said. Kim was shocked for a moment but said nothing.

CHAPTER 19

Ernie put on a surgical mask and fastened a black bandana over his hair, which matched his black clothing. He put surgical goggles on and checked his reflection in the rear-view mirror. His identity was hidden beneath bog-standard PPE. His motorbike was parked four streets away on the Bangor side of the hospital and he removed the PPE to walk to the entrance and then redressed when he arrived. The reception area was deathly quiet, still-in-a-pandemic-quiet. The hospital was still imposing a ban on visitors of any type onto the wards, except those coming to say goodbye to the dying. He made his way through the network of corridors and took the lift to the landing outside the ward where Rio Woods was being treated. His phone call to the ward sister earlier, pretending to be his father, had revealed they were about to release him, so he could go home. He was no longer in danger from his injuries and therefore not a priority. They were concerned about the onset of delayed concussion and he would be given an information sheet, which explained the symptoms, should they arise, but he could be monitored at home. Getting to him at home would be virtually impossible and Ernie wanted a chat with him before he left hospital, just to straighten things out between them, so that Rio was under no illusion that the consequences of harassing Helen any further would be catastrophic. Probably fatal.

He waited in the hallway and studied the cameras and a quick slice with a box-cutter disabled the one covering the toilets. Sure enough, five minutes later, Rio walked from his room to use the public toilets, unaccompanied and unaware of any danger. His face was swollen, and he looked bruised, but he was capable of going to the toilet unaided, so the timing was perfect. It was so quiet, there was little to no chance of being interrupted. They had unfinished business.

Rio glanced in his direction but saw nothing but a security employee, dressed like everyone else, who patrolled the corridors. Rio still had an arrogant swagger, which irritated Ernie. It made his blood boil. The text messages sent to Helen scrolled through his mind, reenforcing the need to act swiftly and decisively. It would be a cold day in hell before that boy put his tongue anywhere near Helen. He waited for Rio to step inside the toilets before following him.

Chapter 20

Rob Wilkinson was waiting for the results to come back with a match. The system was ploughing through its files, trying to find an identical profile. His processing of the evidence had gone well, with multiple clean samples shaved from the piece of scalp and more from the hair roots. Hair roots were forensic gold dust. The blood had been more difficult to work with and had taken longer to separate, but he'd got there in the end and arrived with decent samples to test. He made a coffee and went back to his desk. Pamela was still at the scene and hadn't called with anything interesting yet. There was still no Senior Investigating Officer assigned, which wasn't surprising given the complexity of the case. Two senior detectives were in potentially fatal situations. The SIO would most likely be brought in from a neighbouring force to avoid a conflict of interest, but they would be handpicked and needed to have a proven track record of delivering results. This was the type of case which could make or break a career. Most senior detectives would run a mile in the opposite direction rather than touch it, and he didn't blame them.

His phone rang, and he checked the caller ID. It wasn't recognised but wasn't a spam call either. He answered it in case it was important.

'Rob Wilkinson,' he answered.

'Hello, Rob,' a voice said. He didn't recognise it. 'It's Claire York.'

'Hello, Claire. How can I help?' he asked, frowning. He didn't recognise the name or the voice.

'How are you?'

'I'm fine thanks,' Rob said, still at a loss but not wanting to be rude.

'Do you remember me?' she asked.

'If I'm honest, no.'

'It's Claire.'

'Sorry,' Rob said. 'Claire who?'

'York,' she said. The name rang a bell. Not a good one. Tight Lycra dress, beer belly, and duck-lips but he couldn't remember who she was. He remembered she couldn't get out of the room quickly enough when she woke up in the morning, which had been a massive relief. His beer-goggles had been working well the night before. He thought he'd gone to bed with a fitty not a fatty. 'We met at the GMP Christmas party a few years ago.'

'Ah, that Claire,' Rob said. He had a light bulb moment. 'Claire York from the Manchester Evening News?'

'I'm actually with the BBC news nowadays,' Claire said. 'I was offered the step up and jumped ship last year. It was the best thing I've ever done. How are you?'

'I'm very well thank you but extremely busy.' Rob sighed, tiring of the charade.

'I bet you are,' Claire said. 'Your job must be so interesting.'

'It certainly is… What a coincidence hearing from you today,' he said, rolling his eyes. 'How can I help you, Claire?'

'I was wondering if you fancy going for a quick drink after work this evening?' Claire asked, sheepishly. 'It's time we had a catch-up.'

'Wow. Three years of silence and suddenly, an invite for a drink after work?' Rob said, chuckling. 'I wonder how long it would take before you ask me about the Anglesey case?'

'Aah. Busted. You know how these things go. You scratch my back and I'll scratch yours,' she said, coyly. 'If you still like that kind of thing.'

'Brassy. Very brassy indeed. I thought you had a bit more class than that.'

'Give me a break.'

'Fuck off, Claire.'

'Oh, come on…'

'Goodbye, Claire,' Rob said, hanging up. He blocked her number and sipped his coffee. 'What a twunt,' he muttered. His screen stopped searching. It had found a match and an ID.

'You little beauty,' he said, writing down the details. 'We've got you,' he whispered as he called Pamela.

A Disturbing Thing Happened Today

Chapter 21

Detective Superintendent Olivia Mann was standing in a farmer's field at the arse-end of Saddleworth Moor, Greater Manchester. The rain was falling diagonally, driven by a cutting wind, which roared over the moors and chilled her to the bone. She was wearing a blue forensic suit and wellington boots that squelched in the mud as she approached three bodies, which were naked, bound, and gagged. All three men had been tortured before being shot in the back of the head, execution style.

'Is it them?' Olivia asked one of her DIs, who'd arrived before her. She studied their faces, but the swelling and purple bruising had disfigured them beyond recognition. She couldn't identify them as the men she'd been investigating for months. They had been handsome and rugged and if they'd chosen a different career, they probably could have been pin-ups. The corpses in front of her bore no resemblance to anyone living. The suffering they'd endured had transformed them into something from the darkest pits of hell.

'That's Darren Ring, Craig Eccles, and this one is his brother, Casper,' the DI said, nodding. 'Their teeth and tongues have been removed, fingertips dissolved in acid, toes and genitals taken, probably with a scalpel or another surgical instrument, but their tattoos are intact.' He shrugged. 'Darren has the Manchester City crest on his left shoulder and the blue swallows on his hands between finger and thumb. Craig has his name on his right forearm along with his kids' names, and Casper has this Japanese scene backpiece. It's a bespoke tattoo. We've double checked their records and the ink work matches. Sorry, boss, it's definitely them.'

'Eighteen months of graft down the toilet,' Olivia said, shaking her head. 'We were so close to nailing these tossers and they go and get themselves wiped out,' she added, smiling thinly. 'Inconsiderate bastards.'

'It's an occupational hazard,' the DI said. 'If you step into that world, you take your chances.'

'It looks like they ran out of chances,' Olivia said.

'It's been on the cards for ages. They ripped off so many dangerous characters it was only a matter of time before someone snuffed them out. If you play with fire…'

'They got burnt, all right. Rough justice,' Olivia said, studying them. 'They must have suffered, which is comforting considering how they terrorised people for years and I should be glad they're dead, but I wanted to take them down.' She shrugged. 'Call me a selfish bitch, but I'm pissed off.'

'We were close, boss. That's why they're here.'

'I'm being selfish and insensitive, and I know they have families and children and friends, blah, blah, blah, but I'm disappointed.'

'It saves us a job,' the DI said.

'True,' Olivia agreed. She frowned. 'Whoever managed to take the three of them at the same time knows what they're doing.'

'It did cross my mind,' the DI said.

'Put an alert on their vehicles. I want to know how they got all three of them at the same time,' Olivia said. 'How the fuck did they do that?'

'I'll call it in now.'

'This is a gangland execution, brutal and public, a message to everyone on the wrong side of the law in Manchester, but who had the balls to do it?' Olivia asked herself. 'This would have taken manpower and firepower and somewhere very quiet. Whoever worked them over has done this before many times. Look at the wounds. The cuts are neat, no tearing or sawing marks on the skin, and they had a strong stomach. This guy specialises in information extraction, one-hundred per cent.'

'Maybe someone knew we were close to nailing them, boss,' the DI said. 'Maybe they've been silenced by the upper echelon. Everyone has a boss to answer to somewhere.'

'The Eccles brothers were near the top of the tree,' Olivia said.

'The guys at the top couldn't risk them being arrested and charged with something that would stick. No way.'

'Maybe,' Olivia said. 'If the upper echelon knew we were close to arresting them, it confirms we definitely have a leak.' She shrugged.

'We have a leak,' the DI agreed, nodding. 'No doubt about it.'

'I know we have a leak. Everyone knows we have a leak, but we don't know who the bastard is yet.' She looked at the bodies in silence for a minute.

'We have more than one,' the DI said. 'It pains me to say that, but we have several rats on their payroll. We must have.'

'Until we plug the leaks, we're wasting our time. Every time we get close to lifting anyone of any significance, they'll burn them before we can get to them. They're not going to risk anyone making a deal and turning evidence.'

'We need to step up the pressure on the money men,' the DI said. 'They're the ones calling the shots.'

'We all know the Bartlets call the shots, but we also know they're as clean as the day they were born,' Olivia said. 'There may be a way to implicate them somewhere, but we're nowhere near finding it.'

'Everyone makes mistakes.'

'They let others make the mistakes for them and they make sure there are no connections leading directly back to them.' She shook her head. 'This puts everyone involved in the investigation in jeopardy. Everyone from the ground upwards. We have to assume they were interrogated and, looking at their injuries, they talked.'

'Before they ripped their tongues out.'

'Absolutely no doubt about it. I want all our undercover officers pulled out and debriefed this afternoon. Once we've spoken to them, we'll make a call on who's been compromised and who can return to the field.' She thought for a second. 'And we need to prep all the

CHIS handlers. Their informants are going to be more vulnerable than ever.'

'We're having an issue communicating at the moment,' the DI said, frowning.

'With whom?' Olivia asked, feeling a shiver run down her spine.

'We can't reach any of them.'

Chapter 22

The surgeons had operated on Alan for eight hours stopped the bleeding as best they could, prioritising by the size of the wound. The pellets were removed where possible but some were so deep into the tissue it was better to leave them where they were for now. It had taken nine pints of blood to keep him stable and several litres of plasma to keep his heart beating while they operated, and they were sure he would need a lot more before they're finished removing the shot. He would need several operations over the coming months to get it all. He was made comfortable and wheeled into ICU where he would be kept in an induced coma until they were confident enough to bring him out of it. His body had suffered massive trauma and now it needed a chance to begin the repair and recovery process, which would take years if he lived through the next forty-eight hours. His chances of survival were no more than fifty-fifty, which was better than first anticipated.

His family and friends were not allowed to be there. No one was there when he was attached to the monitors and made as comfortable as possible. His sons had been told not to go to the hospital until they were contacted, which was causing them intense anxiety. They were deeply concerned their dad might not make it. Alan knew they would be worried about him, but in a way, he was glad they didn't have to see him in this state. Deep in the darkest recesses of his mind, where he'd gone to avoid the pain, he was warm and comfortable. His body was broken, but his mind was active beneath the fog of anaesthetic. He wondered about Kim and where she was, and he hoped she was safe somewhere. No one could come and whisper in his ear and tell him she was okay. All his colleagues were busy trying to find out who shot him and kidnapped Kim, so they were unlikely to try to visit. He knew how the force responded to one of their own being hurt or endangered. It was like poking a sleeping bear with a sharp stick. They would be running around day and night until they brought someone to justice, and it gave him a smug satisfaction that he was part of an awesome organisation which kept society safe. It wouldn't rest until they exhausted every avenue to find Kim and the perpetrators who injured him. Not even for a moment.

He didn't feel lonely or neglected, and a strange calm spread through his being. It was a new sensation, and he hadn't experienced anything like it before. He embraced it. Warmth seeped through his nervous system, alerting his brain that his body was shutting down. Through the fog of medication, he was aware that he was badly injured, although the pain was being muted by the drugs and he felt no panic, no anxiety, and no regrets as his heart stopped beating.

CHAPTER 23

Bob and April had waited for ten minutes or so for the head to return when the comms buzzed. The desk sergeant told Bob to ring him from his mobile, which was odd. It must be something that couldn't be broadcasted on an open channel.

'I'll give Dave a call,' Bob said. He scrolled to the number and waited. 'Dave, it's Bob. What's the problem?'

'Are you still working the Rio Woods assault allegation?'

'Yes,' Bob said. 'We're following up on the whereabouts of the man he accused, Ernest Metcalfe, as he's denying any knowledge of the assault.'

'Surprise, surprise.'

'His mother has given him an alibi,' Bob said. 'She says he was at home in bed at the time of the attack and that his daughters were there too, hence the follow up.'

'Where are you?'

'At the school in Bodedern.'

'Don't waste any more time on it. We've just had a call from Ysbyty Gwynedd saying Rio Woods has withdrawn the allegation.'

'What?'

'He says he made a mistake,' the desk sergeant said.

'How can it be a mistake?'

'He's changed his mind and says he isn't sure who attacked him, but it definitely wasn't Metcalfe.'

'What a load of old bollocks. That's very odd,' Bob said. 'There was no doubt in his mind who attacked him when we spoke to him this morning.'

'That's what he's saying now.'

'Who called it in?'

'His mother called the station five minutes ago.'

'Okay,' Bob said. 'He's only fifteen, so what she says goes. We can't force him to press charges. It makes me wonder if he's had any contact with Metcalfe. Do you think there have been any threats at all?'

'That was my first thought. I asked if he'd spoken to anyone while he's been in hospital and his mother said no. She's as confused about it as we are.'

'Surely, he's given her an explanation?'

'Sort of. He thinks the bang on his head confused him and that's why he made the mistake.'

'How did she sound?' Bob asked.

'Embarrassed. She must have apologised a dozen times, but she said Rio has no idea who attacked him and he's adamant he's made a mistake in identifying Metcalfe as his attacker. She said he's been getting very upset that he's accused the wrong man. Apparently, he won't stop crying.'

'Okay. It's all a bit melodramatic for my liking,' Bob said. 'We'll give him a couple of hours to get home and have a think about what he's saying and we'll call and see him first thing tomorrow morning. This doesn't sit right with me, but if that's what he's saying, we'll have to take his word for now. Thanks, Dave. We'll leave the legwork there for today.'

'Okay. I'll message you if we hear anything more.'

'Cheers, Dave,' Bob said. He hung up, and the headmistress entered the room. She smiled and sat down in her chair.

'I've spoken to her,' she said, sighing heavily.

'What did she say?'

'She said that she said goodbye to her father on the way out of the house,' the head said. 'He was having a lie in because he's got a bad back and couldn't take them to school.'

'Okay, thank you,' Bob said, standing. 'We appreciate your help.'

'No problem,' the head said. The officers headed for the door. She looked disappointed. 'Is that it?'

'Yes, that's it,' Bob said. 'It looks like the entire thing has been a misunderstanding.'

'A misunderstanding.' The head was annoyed. 'More like a waste of professional time and time is precious in this school,' the head said, frowning. 'I'm sure you have better things to do. I know I certainly do.'

'We appreciate your help and without going into detail, it has helped with our investigation,' April said. 'It hasn't been a complete waste of time.'

'Glad to hear it. I need to get on. I'm sure you can find your own way out?'

'We'll manage,' Bob said, smiling. 'Thanks again.' They left office and walked through the reception area. 'She's an old battle-axe if ever I met one,' Bob said. They exited the school and Bob turned to April. 'What do you think is going on with the Woods boy?'

'I haven't got the foggiest idea,' April said. 'But I do know he's telling lies.'

CHAPTER 24

Conor and Jimmy Woods walked into the Caernarfon Castle pub, which was situated behind Holyhead Police Station on Cambria Street. It was often used by police officers to unwind with a few pints at the end of their shifts. Wills was already sitting at a table in the poolroom and had three pints of Guinness waiting for them. He beckoned them over with a wave. Jimmy said hello to the landlord, Tommy, and the publican put his finger to his lips and winked. It was obvious Tommy had some information, but couldn't talk because of the police officers standing at the bar. They walked to where Wills was sitting and sat opposite him on a bench seat. Wills was wearing motorbike leathers and had his helmet on the seat next to him. His greying hair was flat to his head in places and spiked like a punk rocker in others; one of the many hazards of riding a motorbike. He had a smug look on his face.

'What are you looking so happy about?' Conor grunted as he sat down.

'I have some news for you.'

'Are you up the duff?' Conor asked.

'No.'

'Are you coming out of the closet?'

'No.'

'Are you in love with Tom Daley?'

'Don't be an arse all your life,' Wills said.

'I give up. Tell us,' Conor said.

'I went into the copshop reception and asked if my brother Ernest Metcalfe was still in custody,' Wills said. He grinned and sipped his stout.

'Okay.'

'I pretended to be his brother,' he emphasised, grinning like a Cheshire cat.

'You've already said that.'

'I had them fooled, because they checked the computer to see where he was. Up here for thinking, down there for dancing,' he said, tapping his head. His companions appeared to be unimpressed and waited for him to expand. 'I could be a gumtree, ye.'

'You mean gumshoe,' Jimmy said.

'What?'

'A gumshoe is a private investigator,' Jimmy said, shaking his head. 'Gumtree is a website for people who've been kicked off eBay.'

'You know what I mean,' Wills said, frustrated.

'If you had two heads, you'd be twice as stupid.'

'No need for that,' Wills said, hurt.

'So, you pretended to be his brother?'

'Yes. Sneaky, ye?'

'Fucking hell. That doesn't make you Jason Bourne, Wills. And?' Conor asked, slurping his pint.

'And what?'

'What did they say, empty head?'

'They said there was no one by that name in the cells or in the interview rooms,' Wills said, whispering. 'The bent fucker isn't even in the station.'

'He's not there?' Jimmy asked.

'Nope. He's not in the nick at all.'

'I wonder why they didn't arrest him?' Jimmy said, shaking his head. 'Surely they would have taken him in. An assault on a young boy like that should be taken seriously, ye.'

'Maybe he's done a runner,' Conor said. 'He might be on a ferry to Ireland by now. I would be if I was a paedo.'

'That would explain why he's not in the cells,' Jimmy said, frowning. He felt a wave of relief wash over him. The thought of planning a violent attack on Metcalfe was giving him anxiety, but he could hardly pull out of it, it was his son that had been assaulted after all. 'It might be for the best,' he added. The look on Conor's face indicated that was the wrong thing to say. 'What I meant to say is, it'll give us more time to plan properly rather than rushing in.'

'I hope you're not getting cold feet?'

'Of course not. Rio is my flesh and blood, but we can't go kicking Metcalfe's head in before we've thought it through.'

'It doesn't take a lot of thinking about in my opinion. He's attacked your son and nearly killed him.'

'I know that.'

'So, what are you worrying about?' Conor asked.

'We don't want to be up on an assault charge too, do we?'

'Assault?' Conor snorted. 'It will be a lot more than assault.'

'How can it be more than that?'

'Listen to me. This pervert jumped out from behind a tree, grabbed your son by his bollocks so hard that it put him in hospital. He butted him and bashed his head against a tree and then tried to drown him.' Conor looked disgusted. 'What kind of freak are we dealing with here?' he asked the entire room. A few people turned to see who was raising his voice but looked away quickly. Conor had a reputation of going off like a firework at the slightest thing. No one made eye contact, but one of the policemen glanced at their faces.

'Keep your voice down,' Jimmy said. 'For God's sake, be quiet about it, will you?' Conor took a deep breath and sipped his beer. 'If anything happens to Metcalfe, they'll be looking at me straight away.'

'Not if they don't find him,' Conor said.

'What are you talking about?' Jimmy said, feeling sick.

'If we do this, we do it properly. We're going to hurt him and then put him where no one will find him.'

'Like where?' Jimmy asked, not wanting to hear the answer.

'Like in the sea,' Conor said, lowering his voice. 'Don't you worry about an assault charge. If we get this wrong, it'll be much worse than that,' he said, slapping Jimmy on the back. 'We can grow old together in Strangeways.' He grinned. 'Before we can do that, we need to know where he is. If he's not in the copshop, where is the fucking bender?'

Tommy, the landlord, approached the table and sat down on an empty stool and smiled. He had the nose of a pugilist and a soft Irish lilt.

'How's it going?' he asked, looking over his shoulder. The officers at the bar were chatting, oblivious to their conversation.

'Okay, thanks, Tommy,' Wills said.

'How's Rio?' Tommy asked. 'I heard what happened. It's a terrible thing.'

'He's battered and bruised,' Jimmy said. 'His todger looks like a tomato chipolata, but he'll live.'

'Poor bugger must be in agony,' Tommy said. 'Do you have any idea why he attacked him?'

'Not really. Rio is friends with his daughter on Facebook, but he's never met him,' Jimmy said. 'It was completely unprovoked.'

'It's a terrible thing.'

'Don't you worry,' Conor said. 'We're going to get payback.'

'Are you indeed?' Tommy said, shaking his head. 'I'd be careful before you go around making threats like that.' He leant in closer. 'I've been listening to our friends in blue chatting at the bar and your boy has changed his story.'

'What?' Jimmy asked.

'They're saying he changed his story and doesn't have a clue who attacked him,' Tommy said. 'Best get your facts straight before you do anything stupid,' he added.

'Who said we're planning to do anything stupid?' Conor asked.

'Everything you do is stupid, Conor,' Tommy said. Conor looked offended but didn't argue. Tommy was older but more than a handful even for a man of his size. 'Take my advice. Speak to your boy tomorrow when his head has cleared and get the full story.'

'I don't know what to say,' Jimmy said, astonished. 'I'm gobsmacked.'

'Listen to me. I've asked around and this Ernest Metcalfe guy is an ex-Army veteran and was RAF police when he left the service. His wife died a few years back in a car accident in the mountains. He lives in the bay with his three daughters and his mother.' Tommy shook his head. 'Something is amiss here. He doesn't sound like the type of man to be a nonce and attack a boy for no reason.'

'They don't have paedo tattooed on their forehead,' Conor grumbled. 'Having kids means nothing. Plenty of nonces have kids. It helps them fool everyone into thinking they're normal.'

'And what is normal, Conor?' Tommy asked, smiling. 'Are you telling me that you're the definition of normal because if you are, we're all fucked.'

'Funny.' Conor snorted. He glared at Wills and Jimmy who were laughing. 'What are you bell ends laughing at?'

'All I'm saying is you need to tread very carefully,' Tommy said. Two new customers walked in. Tommy stood up to go and serve them. 'I'll pour you another pint of the black stuff while you have a little think about it, but mark my words, be careful.'

The three men sipped their beer in silence as Tommy walked away.

'Tommy might have a point,' Wills said.

'What about?' Conor sneered.

'About you not being normal,' Wills said. Jimmy laughed again.

'How about I throw you both through the window?' Conor said, grinning. 'Pair of silly fuckers.' He nodded and lowered his voice. 'Listen to me. Tommy is a nosey cunt, and he likes to interfere wherever possible. He thinks he's the governor of this town,' Conor said, frowning.

'He's a landlord. They hear things, especially when the dibble are in and the ale is flowing,' Wills argued. 'He must hear all kinds of stuff behind that bar. Stuff we'll never know.'

'He's so far up the dibble's arse he could brush their teeth from the inside.' Conor shook his head and emptied his pint.

'Tommy's okay,' Jimmy said. 'He's a good bloke and I trust him.'

'The man is too close to the dibble to be trusted.'

'What are you saying?'

'He's a fucking grass.' Conor lowered his voice. 'Regardless of what he said, we need to find out where Metcalfe is and what his routine is.'

'I need to find out what the fuck's going on and why Rio's changed his story, but he isn't answering his phone,' Jimmy said.

'I thought the paedo stole it from him?' Wills said.

'Oh yes,' Jimmy said, smiling. 'That's why he's not answering.'

'Fucking retard.'

'Let me ask you this question, Jimmy,' Conor said. 'How sure was your boy of who assaulted him when you saw him in the hospital?'

'He was adamant,' Jimmy said.

'There were no doubts?'

'None.'

'So, why the change of tune?' Conor said, shrugging. Jimmy didn't reply.

'He has a point, ye,' Wills said.

'When witnesses change their story, one of two things has happened. First, they were lying in the first instance or second, they've been intimidated or paid to change their statement.' The men looked at each other and nodded in silence. 'I'm telling you now, this stinks to high heaven, ye. He's got to Rio somehow. Your son has been seriously sexually assaulted, and he was certain of who carried out the attack. Suddenly he can't identify his attacker, but he's sure it isn't Metcalfe?'

'It doesn't make sense,' Jimmy agreed.

'No. It doesn't make sense,' Conor said. 'Take no notice of Tommy. He's a fucking snowflake, and it's not his son who was attacked. It would be a different story if it was his child. Tommy acts like butter wouldn't melt in his mouth, but if the shoe was on the other foot, he'd be cleaning his shotgun.'

'I don't know what to think now,' Jimmy said.

'Don't overthink it. We're not going to let that fucking nonce walk away from this, Jimmy.'

CHAPTER 25

Diane Warburton walked into the operations room at Holyhead, which was an event in itself. Most of the MIT were out of the office, but over thirty detectives were gathered there for a briefing. Bill Armstrong was sitting behind Alan's desk. Richard Lewis and Chod Hall were leaning against the desk, making calls and waiting to listen to his brief. The ACC saw his superior coming and stood up, coming out of the office to greet her. He wasn't expecting her, but she had a habit of turning up unannounced.

'You all know Chief Constable Warburton,' he said in introduction. The detectives looked as uncomfortable as he did. Richard straightened his tie and tried to smarten his shirt buttons but failed miserably. Murmured greetings came from the collective.

'Good afternoon, ladies and gentlemen. I want to thank you all for agreeing to work on this. It's a shocking case which reenforces how vulnerable we are as individuals and as a force. We're only human, but when one of ours is in danger, we respond with venom.' Heads nodded in agreement. 'You all look ready for action,' she said, looking around the room. Some of the detectives were already wearing stab vests in preparation for the raids. 'Please bring me up to speed.'

'We're waiting on a second ARU to arrive and then we're set to go,' Bill said.

'Is the first unit in place?' she asked.

'Yes. They've sealed off the area here and here,' he said, pointing to a map on the screen. 'We're in the station here,' he added.

'I know where I am,' she said, smiling. 'But thank you for clarifying it.' The gathering laughed, and the mood lightened a little.

'Of course, you do. My point is, no one is going in or out of the Tanner farm.'

'Run the DNA findings by me again please,' Diane asked.

'The samples taken from the axe, skin and hair, matched the profile of Brandon Tanner,' Bill said. 'He's a thirty-five-year-old with a record for supplying class A's, going equipped, several section 18s, riotous affray, GBH with intent, and the list goes on. He's been in and out of lock-up most of his life and has already served twelve years for his offences. He was released from HMP Liverpool three months ago after serving three of a five-year stint. He went down for fraud and GBH following an investigation led by Kim Davies. Her evidence in court sent him away, and he had a hard time inside. Some of the men involved in the fraud had friends on his wing. He appears to have had several bad 'falls' during his stint, but he never fingered his attackers. He ended up seeing a shrink in there.'

'If he had a hard time, he probably blames us for that. Men like that always find someone else to blame. That's motive,' Diane said, nodding. 'Where is he now?'

'He has a farm outside Bryngwran,' Bill said. 'With a workshop where he prepares lorries and vans for MOTs, welding, and the such.'

'The booby trap was welded, wasn't it?' she said.

'Yes. He's more than capable of carrying out the attack and manufacturing the booby trap and he has a history of possessing unlicenced shotguns.' Bill pointed to Chod. 'Chod is from the island and knows him better than anyone. He's had several dealings with him.'

'I've known him since he was a teenager. He's an unstable character,' Chod said. 'He can fly off the handle at the slightest remark, and violence is his first response to most situations he's not happy with.' Chod changed the images on the screen. Photographs of eight men appeared. Most of the images were taken in the custody suite. 'These are his known associates, but only two of them are currently out of jail. Philip Janus and Oscar Kent. Both of them went down for the fraud case, but they received shorter sentences than him. Janus moved away from the island when he came out and is registered as living in Bethesda, while Kent has a bedsit in town above the old Wild West burger shop.' Diane and Bill looked confused. 'Sorry. It's here,' he said, pointing to the map. 'That's literally across the road from here down Boston Street.'

'Near the car park and the church?' Diane asked.

'That's the one,' Chod said. 'Sorry, ma'am. I grew up here. The Wild West was a landmark when I was a teenager. It's force of habit, I'm afraid.'

'Not a problem. Local knowledge is important, especially in a case like this.' She turned to address the room. 'I've requested a senior officer from Greater Manchester Police to take over as SIO. Her name is of no consequence for now, but she's a Detective Superintendent in their serious crime division.' Murmurs rippled through the room. 'She'll be working directly beneath Bill and me, and she'll need every bit of support and local knowledge you can give her.' Nodding heads acknowledged her request. 'Are we bringing Kent and Janus in simultaneously with Tanner?'

'Yes.'

'Have we had obs on them today?'

'Yes,' Chod said. 'Kent is at home and a uniform unit from Bangor has eyes on Janus's house but haven't seen him yet.'

'What about Tanner?'

'His vehicle is outside the farmhouse. We know he's got a head injury and we're assuming that he's there and hoping Kim is there unharmed.'

'Fingers crossed. Risk assessments?' Diane asked.

'They are detailed and complete. They could all be armed and are dangerous,' the ACC said. 'We're going to proceed with extreme caution.'

'Good,' Diane said. 'I'll ride with you.' She gestured to his office. 'I need a quick chat,' she said. 'In private.'

Bill and Diane went into Alan's office and closed the door. Neither sat behind the desk, choosing to stand.

'Is anything wrong?' Bill asked. Worried by her unannounced visit and the request for a chat. 'Quick chat' was code for a bollocking.

'There was an incident in Caernarfon this afternoon,' Diane began. 'It will be all over the news by late evening, but the connection hasn't been made yet.'

'Connection to what?' Bill asked, confused. 'I haven't been made aware of anything relating to our case?'

'Belinda Preece, a crown court judge, and Melisa Wildling were killed in a hit and run earlier this afternoon.' Bill looked shocked. 'They were walking near the walls when a transit van mounted the kerb and struck them. Witnesses said the van was accelerating when it mounted the kerb, which makes it look like it was intentional. The vehicle didn't stop, and we haven't traced it yet.'

'Who's dealing with it?'

'Caernarfon CID have it for now,' Diane said. 'I don't want it linked with this case until it has to be.'

'But it clearly is connected?' Bill mused, frowning. 'Surely, it's too much of a coincidence not to be.'

'For now, they're separate incidents,' Diane insisted. 'I've told Caernarfon to look at cases linking Alan and Kim where Belinda Preece was the presiding judge or Melisa Wildling was at the bench, either prosecuting or defending. She did both.'

'That's going to be quite a few cases,' Bill said. 'At least it might narrow the list down.' Diane looked at him with a stern expression on her face. 'If the cases were linked, of course.'

CHAPTER 26

Roxy could hear the sound of a power tool whirring, quickly followed by the muffled screams of whichever poor soul it was being used on. They were begging for the pain to stop and jabbering incoherent sentences, interspersed with names. Some she recognised, some she didn't. The interrogator's voice was relentless, asking one question after another. Who, what, where, and when, over and over again. The howls of pain and anguish were an abomination on the soul of anyone who heard them. Listening to another human being suffering such agony was abhorrent, and she'd never been so frightened in her twenty-eight years on this planet because she was probably next. When she arrived, there had been others in the stinking dank room, which was so cold her fingers and toes were numb and her body shivered uncontrollably. One by one they'd been taken screaming from that terrible place and subjected to the horrors of the interrogator and his array of electric gadgets, each with its own pitch and tone. Her imagination filled in the gaps: drill, jigsaw, paint-stripper heat gun, grinder, and so on. It was unthinkable that one human could use such items to destroy the body and spirit of another. Roxy tried to block out the screams, but it was impossible.

Roxy wasn't her real name, and she couldn't understand anyone calling their daughter by it. It had a bad girl stigma attached to it.

Roxanne, you don't have to put on the red light…

Sting and The Police had ensured an entire generation and beyond associated the name with the dark underbelly of society, drug addiction, and prostitution. She hated the name, but her handler had given it to her when she decided to become an undercover. It was a decision she'd given lots of thought to before making the jump from uniform into the shadowy world of the UC officers. Her time in uniform had been frustrating and unsatisfying. She joined the force to make a difference and have a positive effect on society and she felt being in uniform was impeding her ambitions and that she was achieving nothing. There were too many obstacles in the way. Red tape, politics, backstabbing, misogynism, and staff shortages stopped her doing the job how she felt it should be done. So, she made the move into the dangerous world of being a UC, cosying up to the most dangerous members of society and informing on them. What could possibly go wrong?

Another agonising scream sent shivers through her. It would be her turn soon, and she felt like her heart was going to explode. The anticipation of being subjected to a prolonged attack by a coke fuelled psychopath with a hammer drill was absolutely unbearable. She wanted to piss her pants at the thought of one second of the pain. She would tell them everything they wanted to know to avoid the agony, but if they already knew she was a UC, they would cut her to pieces for the fun of it. The first rule of interrogation is to make the subject feel like their information is useless. The interrogators make the subject believe they already know everything but need the subject to confirm what he knows. That way, the subject can deal with the guilt of informing quickly. Pain is simply an incentive to part with the information they already know. Roxy didn't know anything they didn't know already. She was sure of that.

Suddenly, the screaming stopped and everywhere fell silent. Then she heard voices and the sound of laughter. A door opened, and she heard something heavy being dragged along the corridor. The coppery smell of blood reached her, followed by excrement and urine. Her breath was stuck in her lungs. She couldn't move. Footsteps approached her.

'Well, well, well,' a voice said. 'Little Roxy the coke whore is actually a pig. Who would have thought that?' Roxy couldn't breathe. 'Take her in. Let's see what else she can tell us about her informers.'

CHAPTER 27

Olivia Mann was summoned by the ACC and her chief superintendent, which only happened when a shitstorm was brewing. They were waiting in the ACC's office and when she walked in, the mood was sombre. The ACC could hardly look her in the eye, but then she never could. She was a sour-faced bitch at the best of times, and Olivia remembered her first sergeant saying she'd fallen from the ugly tree and hit every branch on the way down. She hadn't met her at that stage in her career, but it stuck with her. When she finally met her, she was disappointed, expecting a female Quasimodo dragging her knuckles along the floor behind her, but she was far from ugly. A little plain maybe, but nothing that couldn't be improved with lip fillers and decent lashes. They would improve things dramatically, but she clearly wasn't a fan of cosmetics. Her attitude to other female officers was appalling yet she was renowned for overcommunicating with her male colleagues and her extracurricular activities were the stuff of legend. She was often the subject of station gossip, and it was mostly derogatory.

Olivia sympathised with anyone who was the subject of station jibes, especially personal stuff. The men could be chauvinistic bastards when they got their teeth into some juicy gossip revolving around sex. Whispers would travel very quickly, each person adding their own twist to the plot. A drunken shag on a work function could haunt you for the rest of your career. She had seen the effect it could have on her colleagues, and it wasn't pretty. The nature of the job they did engendered dark humour and the ability to see the funny side of everything, including subjects most of society would consider taboo. It was a coping mechanism but could sometimes be crude, cruel, and cutting. She sensed Jennifer had been the subject of ridicule since her childhood. Her name hadn't helped her to avoid the bullies in the schoolyard or as an adult. Jennifer Dick. As childish as it may seem, people found it funny. To make matters worse, she was often referred to as Jet-Wash-Jenny because of the amount of dick she received; it appeared she wasn't choosy and would drop her draws for anyone with a pulse. Years before, on a stag doo, a young constable had said she'd need her fanny jet-washed before he would consider going near her sexually. The nickname had stuck.

All that aside, her attitude to fellow female officers had been scrutinised on several occasions. Rumour had it her low moral standards had kept her rising through the ranks and on occasion, from being disciplined. Olivia thought she was overcompensating for a difficult experience growing up. Aesthetically, she had not been gifted and being called Jenny Dick had probably caused her to be bullied at school, college, and university. Olivia was sympathetic to her plight, as she was the total opposite. She was ridiculously attractive, with long blond hair and eyes that mesmerised, and she was articulate and intelligent. Getting on in life was so much easier for beautiful people. That was the sad truth about society. People are taken at face value and judgements made in the first few seconds of meeting them. Instincts are undeniable and it is only education and civilisation which tempers those feelings. While she had sympathy for her, Olivia had been on the wrong end of Jet-Wash-Jenny's wrath on several occasions. The attractive female detectives seemed to be treated more harshly, as if she was punishing them for being pretty. Olivia almost felt sorry for her despite her rank, salary, and pension, but she wouldn't like to swap places with her, not for a microsecond. Being called Jet-Wash-Jenny behind her back by an entire division showed she had improvements to make on a relationship level.

'You asked to see me?' Olivia said, without smiling. There was no point in trying to lighten the mood. Jet-Wash-Jenny could suck the joy out of the atmosphere of a small planet without saying a word. Her expression today was fixed in bulldog-chewing-a-wasp mode.

'I did,' Jet-Wash said, nodding. 'Another colossal waste of taxpayers' money, I see?' She looked at Olivia for the first time, her face stern.

'I'm sorry,' Olivia said, frowning. 'Have I walked in part way through a conversation as I haven't got a clue what you're talking about?'

'We were discussing the executions on Saddleworth Moor,' the chief super said, intervening quickly. She was Barbara Reed and Olivia liked her. She was fair and frank and didn't bullshit anyone.

'I see,' Olivia said. 'Was that what you were referring to as a colossal waste of taxpayers' money?' she asked the ACC.

'It was.'

'Because the Eccles brothers are dead?'

'Yes. Of course.'

'Do you think by running the investigation differently I could have influenced their killer's decision to capture, interrogate, torture, and murder them?' Olivia asked, frowning. She was at tipping point, butterflies in her belly and anger bubbling. She was in danger of saying something career-ending. 'I'm interested in where you think I went wrong.'

'It's academic now,' Jet-Wash said, glaring at Olivia. 'The investigation has cost a fortune so far and is now a waste of taxpayers' money.'

'The way I see it, it's quite the opposite,' Olivia said. The ACC blushed red with anger. 'We were weeks away from arresting them. Can you imagine the cost of the operation we were going to carry out to arrest those three men and their associates?' She counted on her fingers as she spoke. 'I would have been coming to you asking to simultaneously carry out a minimum of fifty arrests. We were looking at using at least six armed units, eight forced entry units, over two-hundred uniformed officers, sixty detectives, thirty traffic officers to seal off the roads and make them safe, and the fire brigade and ambulances on standby, that's before we count numerous officers at custody suites in different stations across the borough and that's before they were remanded and locked up waiting for trial dates.' Olivia stopped for a breath.

'The costs would have been eyewatering,' Barbara agreed, trying to calm the situation. 'We can't deny that.'

'Then the trials would have run into the millions with no guarantee of convictions,' Olivia continued. She shrugged. 'From the taxpayers' perspective, whoever rubbed them out has saved us a fortune and removed the possibility of them walking free on a technicality.' She paused but got no response. 'Not to mention the manner of their deaths has probably dissuaded a lot of wannabies from following in their wake. From a budget perspective, you must feel like you've won the fucking lottery.'

Long seconds of silence followed. Olivia had vented and felt emotionally drained.

'It's a sad reflection on where we find ourselves these days,' Barbara said, trying to balance the debate. 'Everything has a cost attached to it and sometimes, we can't afford to persist with some investigations, even when it would be morally right to do so.'

'An interesting take on the matter, but somewhat naïve.' The ACC shuffled some papers and blushed again. 'I've taken your points on-board.'

'Naïve. Which bit did I get wrong?' Olivia asked.

'I'll look forward to reading your report,' the ACC said, nodding, ignoring her question. She deemed the question impertinent and below her. 'Be sure to include a detailed breakdown of your costings to date, please.'

'No problem,' Olivia said, straight-faced. 'I'll do that. Can you enlighten me as to which bit I got wrong, please?'

'Don't push your luck,' Jet-Wash warned.

'Just for future reference,' Olivia said, stony-faced.

'We'll draw a line under the subject for now.'

'As you wish. Is that all?' Olivia asked, smiling coldly. 'Or was there something else you wanted to discuss?'

'A little bird tells me you can't contact our UCs and our Source Team may have been compromised?' Jet-Wash said, tilting her head slightly.

'An assassination on this scale sends shock waves far and wide.' Patronising fucker, Olivia thought. 'It's not uncommon when a paradigm shift like this happens in the underworld,' Olivia said, trying to sound as patronising as she could in return. 'Everyone scurries for cover, including UCs and our CHIS. We're doing everything we can to bring them in.'

'I'm sure you are and I'm sure they're fine. We need to discuss something else with you,' Barbara Reed said, changing the subject. 'We've had several phone calls today asking for you to be seconded to North Wales Police as the SIO of a very sensitive case.'

'You must be joking?' Olivia frowned and shook her head. She had too much to do tidying up the case she was already working on. 'I can't walk away from the Eccles case.'

'They're both dead,' Barbara said. Olivia was going to speak but she held up her hand. 'Hear me out. Two detectives have been attacked, one is in surgery with shotgun wounds and the other, DI

Kim Davies has been kidnapped. The Chief Constable of NWP has asked for you by name to be the independent SIO on the case.'

'Why me?' Olivia asked.

'That's what I said,' Jet-Wash muttered, shaking her head. 'It's beyond me why she's asked for you in name.' Olivia could feel her blood boiling again.

'Bill Armstrong is the ACC over there. He obviously rates you very highly. Your reputation has travelled well,' Barbara said, ignoring the ACC's comments. 'This could be good for your career,' she added.

'That's debatable,' Jet-Wash said. That was the final straw. Bitch.

'You say two detectives were attacked?' Olivia asked.

'Yes. The first was kidnapped, and the second walked into a booby trap at her home when he realised she was missing. He was hit with both barrels of an adapted shotgun. It's unlikely he'll survive his injuries.'

'Any leads?'

'Nothing obvious yet.'

'When do they need me?' Olivia asked.

'Today,' Barbara said. 'They have a DNA hit on a possible suspect, and Bill Armstrong is running things at the moment. You remember Bill, don't you?'

'Yes. He was with the gang unit.' Olivia said, nodding. 'Where do they want me based?'

'Holyhead Police Station,' Barbara said. 'Is that a yes?'

'I'll nip home and pack a bag,' Olivia said, looking at Jet-Wash Jenny. 'This could be good for my career,' she added. The ACC looked up and glared at her. 'If there's nothing else, I'll be on my way. There's no time to waste on cases like this.'

'I'll call Bill and let him know,' Barbara said. 'Good luck and drive carefully.'

****

The crash team got to Alan quickly, and he was uncannily aware of what was happening around him. He could hear anxious words being exchanged as they prepped him for the paddles. Someone called, 'clear' and he felt a shock hit his chest. His muscles spasmed and his teeth felt on edge. If he could have spoken, he would have told them to fuck off and leave him alone. The peaceful and pain-free place he was in was ripped away from him and the agony of being alive returned with a bang. Blinding light streaked through his brain. It was a brutal transition from the tranquillity of near death, back to living. Pain coursed through his body and another electric shock made his muscles spasm and he felt like his nerve endings had burst into flames. He wanted them to stop and let him drift off into the inky blackness where his mind was at peace, but another powerful shock jarred his heart back into action. His lungs sucked in cold air and his body began to function again. He felt helpless and frustrated that they'd dragged him back and he had never been so disappointed in all his life.

Chapter 28

Olivia drove her black Audi A3 towards Eccles where she lived. It was ironic that the brothers she'd investigated bore the same name as the place she lived. The traffic was as shit as it always was. Traffic lights every few hundred yards made every journey a headache. She dialled Dale again, but he wasn't picking up. He said he was working in the city and wouldn't be back until after six. When she'd left that morning, he seemed unusually polite. Not that he wasn't polite normally, but there was something odd about his behaviour. He was being too nice. She'd taken the call from her DI at about eight, telling her the Eccles brothers had been assassinated and dumped on Saddleworth Moor and that meant she wouldn't be home until later that night, probably the early hours of the morning. He moaned if she had to work late, which was the norm, but he spent an inordinate amount of time working after hours himself. The relationship had become mundane, and the highlight had been the new kitchen they bought the year before. Covid and work commitments had stopped them from travelling on holiday and things in the bedroom had fizzled out, too.

He would flip his lid when he heard that she had to go to Wales to work. The green-eyed monster lurked within him and there had been several uncomfortable exchanges in the last twelve months when he had accused her of screwing someone at work. What else could she be doing when she wasn't home until the early hours? He was immature at the best of times, but almost adolescent after a few pints. The Anglesey case would not be wrapped up quickly. A case like this would probably take a few months to clear and she would have to sort out temporary accommodation in a hotel or guest house and Dale would have to visit when he could. There would be no days off or weekends for her for a considerable time.

Olivia turned the corner into their street and saw Dale's Evoque on the drive. That was unusual, especially as he wasn't picking up his phone. His partner at the estate agents, which he owned, sometimes picked him up if they had a meeting with an important client and they were both required to attend, but he hadn't mentioned anything. His partner, Margo, was a very attractive black woman of Nigerian heritage and was married to a six-feet-nine basketball player from Cameroon. As she approached, she saw Margo's Porsche parked on the street. The hairs on her neck tingled, and she felt her guts twist, deep down inside her where worry begins.

When she walked into the house, she could hear music playing, but it was muffled and faint. Definitely upstairs in the bedroom at the rear of the house. Downstairs was as it should be, but Margo's coat was on the settee, next to her car keys and handbag. Her phone was on the coffee table next to Dale's. That was why he wasn't picking up. She took off her shoes and crept up the stairs, dreading what she was going to walk in to. The music was louder, but didn't mask the familiar sounds of Dale fucking. He had a grunt similar to a donkey baying. Margo was equally enthusiastic, encouraging him to do it harder. There was no doubt about what they were doing. Dale had obviously taken the opportunity of having an empty house all day to fuck his partner in their bed. Her heart sank to her feet, and she felt sick, but anger kept her from walking away. How long had they been fucking? Why did that matter?

She needed to see it for herself, just to be sure it wasn't all a bad dream. The panting and gasping noises were becoming increasingly frantic, and she felt she needed to get into the room before anyone had an orgasm. There was no way they were having the satisfaction of climaxing and staining her new sheets. Cheeky bastards. She pushed open the door and switched on the video on her Samsung. Margo was on her hands and knees, facing the door, taking it from behind. They both saw her enter the room at the same time, and the expression on their faces was priceless. If she hadn't been completely heartbroken, she would have found it funny.

CHAPTER 29

Kim was taken into a room frozen in time. It looked like no one had been there for decades. It had been a storeroom of some kind and a section of it had been a workshop in the distant past. Pigeonhole shelving units were fixed to the walls, the wood dry and cracked and covered in a thick coating of grey dust. There was a workbench with a rusted vice at one end. Gossamer webs hung like trailing plants from the corners of the ceiling and the unwholesome odour of damp and mould filled the air. A single bulb illuminated the dank space, struggling to reach the corners of the room. An upturned fruit crate had been made into an impromptu desk on which they'd placed a laptop. A rickety old chair was nearby but looked unfit to bear any weight. They took her to it and gestured for her to sit down. Kim sat on the chair and felt the legs give a little. She waited for the wood to crack, but it held.

'Is she there?' a female voice asked. It came from the laptop. She had the same Irish lilt as Pighead.

'Yes,' Pighead replied. He aimed the camera at Kim. 'Can you see her?'

'Yes. I can now,' the woman said. There was a pause, probably while she looked at Kim although Kim couldn't see her. 'DI Davies, you don't know me and if I told you my name, you probably wouldn't know of me, so there's no need for introductions,' the woman said. 'What you need to know is that I'm a businesswoman with unscrupulous morals and the reason you're here. There is nothing I won't do to protect my interests, family, and friends, including kidnapping a detective. Whether you're found alive or not found at all is completely down to you. Answer my questions honestly and you may live. Don't and you will not see the light of day again. Are we clear?'

'Yes,' Kim said. She sensed the woman was anxious and angry, but there was something else in her tone. There was a sense of menace. Kim could hear it in her voice. 'I understand completely.'

'Good. Let's not beat about the bush. You were involved in the arrest of Leonard O'Malley at the truck stop in Holyhead a few months ago,' the woman said. Her accent was definitely from southern Ireland, but not Dublin. Kim couldn't place it. 'Leonard O'Malley. Do you remember him?'

'Yes, but it was more like eight or nine months ago,' Kim said. 'He had a truck full of Afghans and was aiming to sail on the Dublin ferry.'

'That's him. You were acting on information received from an anonymous source,' the woman said, but it wasn't a question. It was a statement of fact. She had clearly done her homework.

'Yes. The information came from headquarters,' Kim said. 'Most seizures of drugs or people being trafficked come from tipoffs. They're rarely found by a random stop.'

'The word 'tipoff' makes it sound anonymous, but it wasn't an anonymous source, was it?'

'I'm not sure what you mean?' Kim said.

'The information was gleaned via the Source Team in Colwyn Bay,' the woman said. Again, it wasn't a question. She clearly knew the answer.

'That's right.'

'So, it wasn't anonymous.'

'As far as I know, it came via a CHIS, which means the source is anonymous to everyone but their handler,' Kim said. 'Even the other members of the Source Team wouldn't know who it came from.' The woman remained silent. Kim felt her anxiety growing. She felt the need to fill the silence and explain herself. 'Each CHIS is given a name which could be male or female such as Pat or Sam or George with a generic surname such as Jones or Williams, and an identity number. Once the name is applied to their identity number, they are only ever referred to as initials. So, Sam Jones would be SJ in conversation and none of the team would know if they were male or female except their handler and their details are never entered into our computers. Their identities cannot be stumbled across or searched for. They're kept as hard copies in a safe, which only the senior officer of the Source Team has access to.'

'Do you think I'm stupid, Kim?' the woman asked.

'No.' Kim swallowed hard. There was evil intent in the woman's voice. She could sense it. 'I'm just explaining how it works with any CHIS. Their information is as anonymous as it can be. I don't think you're stupid at all.'

'Good. I know how a Source Team works, but thank you for the explanation,' she said. 'Let's be more specific, shall we?'

'Okay.'

'Every handler in the Source Team has an area to cover, don't they?'

'Yes. But it's not set in stone.'

'Meaning?'

'Sometimes disputes happen and a CHIS will request a different handler and if they're deemed to be a valuable asset, we'll oblige the request. Handlers can have assets all over the area we cover.'

'Don't muddy the water, DI Davies.'

'I'm not trying to,' Kim said. 'I'm giving you a clear picture of how we work.'

'But handlers generally cover one area, don't they?'

'Generally, I suppose,' Kim agreed.

'So, stop fucking me around,' the woman said.

'I'm not trying to.'

'Good. Keep it that way.' The woman paused to let her words sink in. 'Which area did the information come from?'

Kim sensed the woman already knew the answer. It was in her voice. She felt like she had laid a trap. 'As far as I'm aware, it came from the island,' Kim said. The woman stayed silent. Kim swallowed hard. She was waiting for more. 'Most CHIS activity is centred in one town, so most likely the Holyhead area.'

'I know how towns like that are. I'm from a small fishing town in the south,' the woman said. 'What's the population of Holyhead?' she asked. Kim knew that she already knew the answer.

'Just over eleven thousand,' Kim said.

'Nothing is anonymous in a town that size,' the woman said. 'Everyone knows everyone, and everyone knows everyone's business.'

'Pretty much.'

'Using your local knowledge, where do you think that information came from?'

'I would be guessing,' Kim said. 'It would be pure speculation.'

'I realise that. I want your best guess.'

'Looking at it logically, I know the information came from someone with contacts in the port, which narrows it down a little.'

'They're bribing people?'

'It happens,' Kim said.

'There are people who turn a blind eye for money in all walks of life.' The woman paused. 'Even yours.'

'Everyone has a price,' Kim said.

'Including you?'

'No. Not me,' Kim said. 'I would leave the job before I stooped so low.'

'Very admirable,' the woman said. 'Tell me more about the bribes.'

'We thought it was probably someone who'd been cut out of the deal and they spilt the beans as recompense. O'Malley took the hit.'

'So, it was an insider?'

'I could hazard a guess, but Leonard O'Malley would have a better idea than me. You've kidnapped a detective inspector? Surely, you have the ability to ask him these questions directly?'

'Unfortunately, Leonard O'Malley has vanished into witness protection,' the woman said. 'He was looking at a long stretch for trafficking and now he's disappeared, so it doesn't take a brain surgeon to work out what he's done. He must be laughing at us all now.'

'I don't know anything about him making a deal,' Kim said. 'After the initial interview, he was handed over to the detectives from GMP.'

'That's not quite true, is it?'

'As far as we were concerned, it was. We were told he was going to Manchester, and he was taken from Holyhead to the cells in St Asaph to wait for a transfer. What happened then is a mystery to me and rumours are he was taken from there by officers from the NCA, but I have no idea if that's true,' Kim said, shrugging. 'We were never party to who took him, where they took him to, or why he was so important. Even if we asked where he was taken to, they wouldn't tell us. They trust no one, not even other police officers.'

'My own experience tells me they're right not to trust you. I know how much it costs me to keep the Garda off my back.' The woman paused. 'I think Leonard was working with someone on the island,' the woman said. 'I think he got greedy and so they turned him in.' Kim didn't comment. 'Leonard was a clever boy, and he had his fingers in several pies and we think he's giving away all the recipes in return for immunity and a new identity.'

'If he is, I wouldn't know anything about it,' Kim said.

'Who was the CHIS handler?'

'For the island?' Kim asked. She was stalling. Her head was telling her to answer the question, but her heart was loyal to her colleagues. She was certain the woman knew the answer, anyway. It wouldn't take long to identify the members of the Source Team. 'Do you mean which officer covered Anglesey?'

'Yes. That's where we are talking about, isn't it?'

'She's a DS called Lorraine Bannerman, based at Colwyn Bay,' Kim said. She didn't think she was telling her anything she didn't already know and so it wasn't betrayal. 'But I think you know that already.'

'Do you know her?'

'Not on a personal basis,' Kim said. 'We've talked on the phone before she went into the ST, but not since.'

'Is she bent?'

'The Source Team officers are selected carefully,' Kim said. 'Any question marks over her honesty would be a barrier to her being selected for that team. ST officers are deemed as trustworthy, without question.'

'Not necessarily,' the woman said. 'Recent events in Manchester would prove your theory wrong. Information from within the force has led to a reshuffle of the major players.'

'I'm not sure what you mean.'

'Have you ever heard of the Eccles brothers?'

'From Manchester?'

'Yes.'

'I've heard them mentioned,' Kim said. 'I know they run most of Manchester and their county lines activities came onto our territory before lockdown. Most of their dealers in North Wales were arrested as part of Operation Josephine a few years back.'

'They've ceased trading,' the voice said. 'Permanently.' Kim understood what she meant.

'Wow,' Kim said. 'One of the hazards of the job, I suppose.'

'They were interviewed by some very nasty people before they retired. They gave away some eye-opening information before they died,' she added. 'Some of it mentioned Leonard O'Malley and his associates.'

'He seems to be a thorn in your side,' Kim said.

'Not anymore,' the woman said. 'Once they've milked him for everything he knows, he'll drift into the obscurity of the witness program where no one will recognise him and he'll work dead-end jobs for the rest of his miserable life.'

'It's better than being dead, I suppose,' Kim said.

'It's the nearest thing to being dead. Leonard O'Malley can't be Leonard O'Malley anymore.'

'I doubt he would live very long if he tried to be,' Kim said. 'Sometimes people in witness protection get so bored with their new lives, they try to come back. We try to dissuade them. It never ends well.'

'I really hope Leonard plans to return when the dust settles. That would be a huge mistake, but one I would enjoy very much.' The woman sounded bitter. 'However, his associates are a concern to me, especially the ones with a penchant for informing to the police. I'm sure you understand what I mean?'

'Yes, but I'm not sure how I can help you,' Kim said. She felt like she was being lead a merry dance, but she didn't know why.

'I want you to tell me who the connected people are in Holyhead. The people who know everything and everyone and wouldn't think twice about informing to keep their liberty or the police looking the other way to protect their own interests.'

'There is no way I could know for sure where that information came from,' Kim said. 'It would be guesswork at best,' she added.

'Try it. It might save your life.'

'There was a time when most of the information was coming from inside. Operation Josephine wiped out an entire network and locked them up. They were spread all over the country and were pissed off with the people who saw the opportunity to take over while they were locked up. The people who stepped into their shoes were plagued by information being leaked to the police and the press. They never got a hold on the supply chain and that was no accident.'

'Who was the leak?'

'There were several all associates of Jake Randall.'

'He's dead,' the woman said.

'Technically, he's missing,' Kim said.

'He's dead,' the woman reiterated.

'We think so, but there's never been a body.'

'There's been no activity on his bank accounts or phones for over a year,' the woman said. 'He's dead and you know it, so it can't be him.'

'I honestly can't say with any certainty where that information came from.'

'Who was working with Leonard O'Malley?'

'I don't know,' Kim said.

'How many people do you know who are capable of working at that level of organised crime and who would be trusted with operational information by an OCG?'

'A handful at best,' Kim said. 'They wouldn't be part of any local crew.'

'Why not?'

'They're too volatile and internal disputes go back generations. A friend one week is an arch enemy the next. My instinct tells me they're from away.'

'There have been some major investigations there over the years,' the woman said.

'Yes, but only as part of wider operations,' Kim said. 'Anglesey is a sleepy community mingled with tourists. Any players on the island are just appendages to the serious outfits in the cities. There are no OCGs in North Wales, just associates. I think you're barking up the wrong tree.'

'I want names. Think carefully, DI Davies.'

'Are you asking me to give you names of people it might be?'

'I'm asking you to use your professional knowhow to narrow it down,' the woman said. 'You were on the O'Malley arrest, and you conducted his interview, so you have a hunch who turned him in, don't you?'

'At the time, I did,' Kim said, uncertainly. 'But with hindsight, it could just as easily come from inside.'

'But we've established the information came via a CHIS from Holyhead?' The woman sighed. 'You're disappointing me, DI Davies. I was hoping that you would want to live.'

'I do,' Kim said, shaking her head. Her heart began to beat faster. 'Of course, I do.'

'I want names,' the woman said. 'Or you go back into the darkness to rot.'

'This is so fucked up. You're asking me to make a guess!'

'An educated guess, detective.' There were a few seconds of silence. 'Okay. Put her back in her tomb.'

'Wait!' Kim shouted. 'Andrew Thornton,' Kim said, panicking. 'My boss and I thought he was involved in the people smuggling ring that was busted three years ago, but there wasn't enough on him to make an arrest.'

'Why him?'

'He had links with some individuals who were using a circus as cover to move people and drugs.' Kim picked her words very carefully. 'He was the first person who came to mind, although I have no evidence to back it up. It could be nothing to do with him.'

'Tell me about Mr Thornton,' the woman asked. Her voice had changed pitch.

'He's from down south, Cambridge way,' Kim said. 'He came to the island about ten years ago, bought two pubs on the island and several houses in Rhosneiger and Beaumaris. The NCA dropped us a line not long after he arrived, warning us to keep an eye on him, which we did, but he didn't put a foot wrong. He knew he was being watched, and he was well behaved, joined the local rotary club and masonic lodge and looked to be a model member of the community.' Kim sipped from her water bottle. 'He fell out with one of his pub managers and he came to us with all kinds of accusations that the pubs were merely a front to launder money. We had no evidence, but it spiked interest in his activities. After a bit of digging around, the NCA told us to back off. They were watching a haulage company based in Brighton with depots in Dover and Felixstowe and Thornton was a major shareholder and advisor to the board.'

'Where does he live?'

'He has a farm with twelve acres on the coast near South Stack,' Kim said. 'He rents most of it out to a neighbouring campsite.'

'Is that his main residence?'

'Yes.'

'Does he work with anyone?'

'He has some business interests with a guy from Bangor called Hurst,' Kim said. 'Everitt Hurst. He was a high court judge before he retired.'

'Write down the name of his farm and his closest associates,' the woman said. Pighead gave her a pen and notepad. Kim scribbled Whitebrook Farm on the page, followed by three names. One of them was Everett, the other two were made up. 'One last question, DI Davies.'

'Go on,' Kim said.

'Niall Kelly,' the woman said. Kim recognised the name but couldn't place it. 'He was arrested on the back of information you shared with the Garda.'

'The name rings a bell,' Kim said, swallowing hard. She wanted to go home. To be safe and warm with a glass of wine and a bar of Galaxy.

'Think hard. Do you remember him or not?' the woman asked. Her tone had hardened. It was almost flat, like monotone.

'I remember him vaguely.'

'Niall Kelly,' the woman repeated. 'You were involved in the investigation on the mainland.'

'Okay. I remember him. What about him?'

'The Eccles brothers parted with some information which is new to me,' the woman said. Kim didn't comment. 'I always thought the Garda had investigated him first, but it turns out, it was you who got him sent away.'

'Me?'

'Yes. You and your boss, Alan Williams were investigating him. Your detectives tailed him to the ferry, and you filmed him during the crossing. He denied ever leaving Ireland, but your evidence put him away.' The woman waited for Kim to process the information. 'Niall Kelly. Remember him?'

'Yes.' Kim was suddenly more frightened. She remembered the case. How could she forget? 'We were tipped off about a weapons cache. Wasn't it something to do with an armed robbery at a security depot?'

'That's it,' the woman said. 'The penny has dropped.'

'That was to do with the Jamie Hollins case years ago?' Kim recalled. 'They planned to rob a depot and sail the money across to the island in ribs,' Kim said. 'It was supposed to be millions?'

'It wasn't about money,' the woman said. 'It was about diamonds. Three million euros worth of bling.'

'I remember it,' Kim said. 'But it wasn't our investigation. It was an Irish job all the way.'

'It was, but it was the testimony from you and your boss, which nailed Niall,' the woman said. 'You both testified by virtual link to the court in Dublin.'

'I'm not sure how you can blame us. He was caught planning to rob an armoured car depository,' Kim said. 'He got caught. How can anyone else be to blame for that?'

'It's a matter of perspective,' the woman said. 'When someone in our business goes to jail, it's the officers in charge who are to blame. In this case, you.'

'That's a very blinkered view,' Kim said. 'Deluded almost.'

'Be very careful.'

'I've been drugged and kidnapped from my own home and now I'm being quizzed while I'm wearing handcuffs,' Kim said. Tears filled her eyes. 'I've never been more careful of what I'm saying in my life, but I really don't see what this has got to do with anything I have done?'

'That's why you're here.'

'I don't understand.'

'Because of you, the Garda followed Niall and focussed their investigation on him. When they arrested him, they found detailed plans of the depository, weapons, and ammunition in his lock-up.'

'I remember it, but once it was with the Garda, we moved onto the next case,' Kim said. 'We don't have time to dwell on cases that move out of our jurisdiction. It became someone else's problem.'

'Niall was unlucky,' the woman said. 'There were others involved. People with much more responsibility for what was planned than him. He was the fall guy. They found automatic weapons and ammunition in his lock-up, which are a huge no-no.'

'Of course, they're frowned upon,' Kim said. 'If they were in his lock-up, he was always in big trouble.'

'Except he didn't have a lock-up,' the woman said.

'They followed him to it,' Kim said. 'So, it became his.'

'They did follow him, but only because you told them about it.'

'We were given information from a source on one of the ferries, which led to the Garda going to a lock-up on the outskirts of

Kilkenny,' Kim said, frowning. 'Obviously, the Garda took the information and ran with it. We had no input on what they did with the information or the investigation.'

'You're missing the point.'

'What am I missing?'

'It wasn't his lock-up.'

'I don't understand?'

'He was on the periphery of a very dangerous outfit, and they have a lot of enemies. They used him to score points and cover their tracks. They fed you false information, and you swallowed it with no consideration for the consequences.'

'We had no way of knowing if the information was good or not,' Kim said, shaking her head. 'It was up to the Irish forces to investigate.'

'Niall got eighteen years because he wouldn't give away any of the others involved.'

'I remember the sentence seemed harsh,' Kim said. 'He was very young. It's always sad when young lives are ruined like that.'

'He was twenty-one when he went down,' the woman said. 'The others involved in the heist were senior members of a paramilitary group and they were worried he might blab when he was caught,' the woman said. 'They made his life in prison difficult to say the least.' Kim had a bad feeling about where the conversation was going.

'I'm sorry to hear that,' Kim said.

'He hanged himself last month, so they say.'

'Oh God, I'm sorry.'

'I think he was hanged by them, and it was made to look like suicide.' Kim remained silent. There was a long pause. 'They silenced him.'

'That's terrible.'

'Terrible?' the woman said. 'He was my son.'

'I'm so very sorry for your loss,' Kim said, her voice hardly a whisper.

'You said you remembered him vaguely,' the woman said.

'I meant the details.'

'You meant my son.'

'I didn't mean any offence by it,' Kim said.

'Was the source who put O'Malley away the same person who told you about Niall and the lock-up?'

'I honestly don't know,' Kim muttered. 'It's possible, I suppose.'

'Not that it matters now,' the woman said. 'When you didn't turn up for work this morning, your boss went to your home to see if you were okay,' the woman said. 'He walked into both barrels of a shotgun.'

'Alan?' Kim muttered. 'Is he alive?'

'Yes, but not for long. He's in surgery, but he's unlikely to make it,' the woman said. 'It's small recompense, but it made me smile.'

'I'm so sorry about your son,' Kim said.

'You will be,' the woman said. 'Put her back in her room. You know what to do with her.'

'What?' Pighead asked, sounding confused.

'Give her something to think about,' the woman said.

'Please don't hurt me,' Kim said, her voice a whisper. Terror seeped through soul.

'You'll have plenty of time to think about Niall and what you did to him before you die.'

'I'm sorry for what happened to your son,' Kim whimpered. 'Please don't put me back in there,' she said, setting her hands in prayer. 'I'm begging you, please don't put me back in there.' Panic set in and tried to stand up. Strong hands lifted her from the chair and her feet kicked at thin air as they took her down the dark, dank corridor. 'I'll tell you anything! Please don't lock me in there.'

'Don't struggle or it will hurt more,' Pighead said. They dragged her down the corridor to the room and lifted her onto the trolley and she began to thrash around. Her head hit one of the guard rails and stunned her. She went limp for a few seconds, long enough for the mask to be slipped over her head. Darkness engulfed her as the zip was fastened and breathing became more difficult. She felt like she was going to choke. Her feet were shackled to the bed, and a restraint fastened around her waist, pinning her down.

'Let me go, please,' Kim begged. She screamed as loud as she could, but her cries were muffled by the mask and her tears. When she could no longer move, the men left, and she heard the light being switched off and the key turning in the lock. As the sound of their footsteps faded, hot tears ran freely down her cheeks, and she sobbed alone in the impenetrable darkness.

Chapter 30

When the forced entry teams simultaneously crashed through the front and back doors of the Tanner farm, there was an air of anticipation, hoping Kim Davies would be found alive and well. The front door team entered a long hallway, tiled with a bright mosaic from the sixties. Threadbare runners ran from the doorway to the kitchen. Two doors to their left accessed a living room and dining room, which had been joined by knocking a wall down. The team split into two units, and one unit moved upstairs in silence.

The back door team entered the kitchen, which was like stepping back in time. It had been designed and fitted in the sixties and smelt of chip fat and bacon. A long oak table had been turned into a makeshift workbench. Three metal generator frames were in the process of being adapted to hold a shotgun, brackets welded to them to carry the weapons and withstand the force of the blast when fired. The teams moved noisily through the kitchen. A smaller unit went downstairs into a cellar. Each room was called clear as they penetrated the building without any resistance. Brandon Tanner was lying in a pool of his own blood on the living room floor. The armed units called the farm clear and allowed the forensic team and detectives to enter.

Diane Warburton and Bill Armstrong were the last officers to enter the building once it had been declared as safe. They were wearing scene suits and overshoes. Armed officers filed out of the farmhouse; their job done. The mood was low and disappointment tainted the atmosphere.

'He's blown his brains out,' the ARU commander said as they approached the living room. 'We're not going to get much out of him.'

'Any sign of Kim?' Bill asked.

'There's no one else here,' the commander said. 'We've checked the attic and the cellar, and the outhouses are being searched as we speak.'

'Thanks,' Bill said, stepping into the room. Tanner was lying on the floor, an ancient revolver in his right hand. The left side of his skull was missing, and the contents were splattered across the wall. They were still wet and gooey, pinkish in colour. 'He hasn't been dead long?' Bill asked.

'He's still warmish. A few hours at least.'

'One side of his head is missing, but there's a deep laceration to the other side.'

'It looks like the axe wound Pamela predicted,' Diane said.

'What the fuck happened here?' Bill asked no one in particular. 'He goes to Kim's home with others as yet unknown, is badly injured during the attack, comes home, and blows his head off.'

'Maybe he knew his injuries would lead us to him,' Diane said. 'If he went to hospital, we'd pick him up immediately.'

'That begs the question, where is Kim?' Bill asked.

'Why was she taken?' Diane asked. 'If they wanted her dead, we would have her body already. So, she was taken for a different purpose.'

'Agreed. Although it's beyond me,' Bill said.

'You need to ask his associates,' Diane said. 'He didn't get here by himself.'

'This doesn't sit right with me,' Bill said, shaking his head.

'Nor me,' Diane said. 'You have a lot to consider here, and you don't need me looking over your shoulder. I'll leave you to it. Call me later with an update.'

Chapter 31

Jimmy Woods knocked on the door and waited for it to be opened; he had butterflies in his stomach. His ex-wife had the ability to make him feel nervous, like a naughty schoolboy waiting to be caned. She was as unforgiving as she was ferocious, with a vocabulary of withering insults few could match.

Experience had taught him to tiptoe around her, especially when she was on one, which was often. His instinct was always to avoid conflict with her as he seldom achieved anything but a humiliating bollocking followed by the silent treatment for forty-eight hours at least but tonight, he needed to speak to Rio. He hadn't been the best father, he knew that, but he did care deeply for his son. Rio was the reason he was still alive and kicking. Jimmy had suffered with depression and alcohol addiction for as long as he could remember. The black dog had bitten him as a teenager and still walked beside him now, and there had been times when suicide was a real option. Sometimes, the only clear option. Rio was the reason he hadn't stepped off the cliff or swallowed the bottle of diazepam he kept in his bedside drawer.

Rio was in trouble and speaking to him face to face was important. It was important enough to risk her wrath. He knocked again and Wendy opened the door long enough to see who it was and then closed it in his face as he tried to step in. She crushed his foot in the door. He withdrew the injured appendage and gritted his teeth against the pain.

'Wendy! You bloody idiot,' he hissed. 'You could have broken my foot.'

'Fuck off,' he heard her shout as the door slammed. 'Knobhead.'

'Open the door, Wendy,' Jimmy said, knocking again. 'I need to speak to you.'

'I'm busy. Fuck off,' Wendy shouted.

'Let me in!'

'You don't live here anymore and nobody in here wants to talk to you.'

'I'm trying to help our son.'

'Oh, now you want to help him?' Wendy said. 'You can't help yourself never mind anyone else.'

'Be reasonable, Wendy.'

'Fuck off!'

'We need to have a family discussion.'

'Oh, you have a family today, do you?' Wendy shouted. 'You're a useless pisspot, Jimmy Woods. Fuck off.'

'I need to talk. It's important.'

'Fuck off.'

'I want to know why Rio's changed his statement.'

'Mind your business,' Wendy shouted. 'Don't pretend you give a toss now. You didn't believe him earlier.'

'Exactly, and now he's withdrawn his complaint,' Jimmy said. 'Something's wrong. I want to talk to you both about it.'

'He doesn't want to talk to you,' Wendy said, lifting the letter box flap. He could see her eyes. 'Fuck off.'

'Grow up, Wendy,' Jimmy said, bending over to look her in the eyes through the flap. Wendy took a mouthful of tea and spat it in his face. 'For fuck's sake!' he shouted, wiping tea from his eyes. 'You stupid cow!'

'Is that grown-up enough for you?' Wendy said, closing the letter box. 'Fuck off.'

'Listen to me, Wendy,' Jimmy said, lowering his voice. 'Conor and Wills are going to do something bad to Metcalfe, and I can't stop them.' Wendy remained quiet behind the door. 'I can't let them hurt him if he didn't do anything,' Jimmy pleaded. 'We could end up in the cells and it would all be for nothing.' Silence. 'Please, Wendy. I need to talk to you and Rio about why he's changed his story. You know what Conor is like. He's nuts, and he's really gunning for Metcalfe.' Silence answered him. 'I don't want to go to jail, Wendy. If anything happens to Metcalfe, I'll be the first person they arrest.' Long seconds passed by. The door opened and Wendy reluctantly let him in.

'You've got five minutes and then you can fuck off.'

****

Ernest Metcalfe had picked up the girls from school and drove into Holyhead to pick up some shopping from Tesco. It was part of their daily routine and they chatted about what lessons they'd done that day and the girls caught up on schoolyard gossip from their respective years, which was more entertaining than it ought to be. Ernie laughed and joked with them, but kept a close eye on Helen. She seemed distracted, as if her mind was somewhere else. Ernie thought she was probably thinking about getting home to go online to see if she had any messages from the Woods boy. Probably. He couldn't be sure what she was thinking, obviously, but he could take a good guess. Just like her mother. Slut.

She was oblivious to the day's events, as she wasn't allowed to look at her phone during school time. She didn't know her father had assaulted her friend, and she also had no idea that her dad had wiped her contacts and closed her Facebook, Instagram, and TikTok accounts. They would need to have a conversation about her departure from social media. It would be a stormy encounter, but it needed to be done for her own good, and it was non-negotiable. He was certain she wouldn't see it that way, but it was his job as a father to ensure her safety, whether she appreciated it or not. Woods wouldn't be bothering her again. He was one-hundred per cent positive about that. He'd taken a big risk approaching him again, but it had to be done. Protecting Helen was his number one priority, even if he had to protect her from herself. She had no idea she was the spawn of a cock-sucking Jezebel. Her mother was the worst type of human being, the type no one could trust. The type who would smile to your face and then open her legs for anyone with a penis the minute your back was turned. Slut.

Helen was the double of her mother, which meant she had her genes and that meant she probably had her mindset too. Little things she said and did reminded Ernie of Naomi, but instead of making him smile, they made his blood boil. He could feel his anger rising and he would have to take himself away from her before he could calm down. He loved Helen with every sinew of his body, and it wasn't her fault she looked like her mother. Slut.

There was no way Ernie could allow Helen to make the same mistakes her mother had. Not while he had breath in his lungs. The risks he'd taken were measured and justifiable in order to keep her innocence and dignity intact, and that meant the police were involved. The police would be back. He was positive of that, too. He was well aware he needed to avoid scrutiny from them. His anonymity was crucial to his survival as a free man. A son. A father. A protector. A murderer. A psychopath.

As a treat, and to delay their arrival at home, he'd taken the girls to Langdons on the Newry for tea. The food was good, and the view of the marina and breakwater relaxed him, and life felt as normal as normal could be for Ernest Metcalfe. The internal storm in his soul calmed for a few hours. His girls were safe and happy and healthy, and all was good with the world. Until he realised the man sitting near the fire escape wearing bike leathers was trying hard not to catch him looking at them. His interest was unnatural. He was jittery and pretending not to notice them. Ernest acted as if he hadn't spotted him, finished his dessert, and paid the bill.

His military training and survival instincts kicked in. The girls were chatting incessantly as they left the restaurant and climbed into the Jeep. Ernie got into the driver's seat and started the engine. He adjusted the heater setting and watched the rear-view mirror. Sure enough, the biker came out of the restaurant and put on his helmet. He glanced at the Jeep a little too long and Ernie caught his eye, just for a second. It was long enough to know his instincts were correct. The man on the bike was surveilling them. He was too amateurish to be police or one of the good guys, which meant he was a bad guy. Things never ended well for the bad guys.

****

Brandon Tanner's associates, Philip Janus and Oscar Kent, were arrested without incident. They were clearly stunned by the level of force used and the number of police officers carrying weapons. Oscar Kent pissed his pants while he was being cuffed. They were asked numerous times where DI Kim Davies was and neither man knew her or her whereabouts. The arresting detectives had brought in enough serious criminals to know when one was lying. It was obvious both men were shitting themselves at the mention of police officers being shot and abducted. Janus was taken to St Asaph and Kent to Holyhead, and both men were tight-lipped and demanding lawyers. Bill Armstrong took the view that letting them sleep on it overnight and interviewing them in the morning was the best way forward. He was convinced neither knew where Kim was and Olivia Mann was en route to head up the case and it would be her call how they approached Tanner's associates. She was due to arrive in the early evening and he would give her a full briefing and ease her into the lead role.

****

Ernie pulled into his driveway and the girls jumped out of the Jeep before he'd turned the engine and lights off. His mother opened the kitchen door and hugged each of them as they stepped inside.

'Oh, how you've grown,' she said, kissing them on the forehead. 'Which one are you?' she asked. 'You've grown so quickly I can't tell who's the youngest.' The girls laughed, despite hearing the same line every time they came home from school. 'Goodness me, what have they been feeding you at that school?'

Ernie listened to them laughing. It was the sweetest sound, but his attention was on the road behind him. He pretended to be routing in the glove box, while watching the mirror. A single headlight approached, the motorbike slowed, and the rider glanced down the driveway. Ernie waited for it to pass before jogging down the driveway to confirm the reg number. He watched as the motorbike took the bend at Craig-y-Mor. It went out of sight, and he listened to the engine disappearing as it went by Porth-y-post and up the hill past the grange. Whoever the rider was, he would be having a conversation with him about why he was following them. The reg plate would lead him to his doorstep. He checked the road in both directions, and it was clear. The lights on Ravenspoint Road twinkled across the bay and the universe twinkled above him like silver jewels against the dark Anglesey sky. It was a beautiful vista, and he took a deep breath and savoured it for a while. The wind picked up from the sea, chilling him, and Ernie headed inside to speak to Helen.

****

Jimmy Woods waited in the kitchen for his son Rio to come downstairs. His mum had asked him to come down to talk to them, politely at first but the exchange disintegrated into a tirade of four-letter words and tears. Wendy had a flair for the dramatic and Rio had inherited it. Jimmy wanted to intervene but knew better of it. They would both turn on him and forget what the spat was about in the first place. It had been the pattern of their lives together as a family up to the point where Jimmy walked out of the family home and never went back. Their relationships were fractured at best, but he did try to maintain cordial communications with both of them. Alcohol didn't help one little bit. Both Wendy and Jimmy were binge drinkers, in denial that there was an issue. Rio stormed down the stairs and through the kitchen before dropping onto the settee, arms folded defensively, face like thunder. Jimmy followed him.

'What the fuck do you want?' he snapped.

'I've come to talk to you about why you've changed your story,' Jimmy said.

'What do you care about it?'

'Of course, I care.'

'You didn't believe me, anyway, so why are you bothered now?'

'I didn't say I didn't believe you, son,' Jimmy said, remaining calm. 'I said the entire thing just didn't add up and now you've changed your story I'm even more convinced something stinks.'

'Just leave it alone,' Rio snapped.

'We can't pretend nothing's happened, Rio,' Jimmy said. 'Something happened and I want to get to the bottom of it before things get out of our control.'

'I fell over, banged my head, and got a concussion. End of story.'

'I don't believe that. Not for one second.'

'Believe what you want. I don't care.'

'Can we have a grown-up conversation about this, please?' Jimmy reasoned. 'You were attacked on your way to school. You didn't fall over.' Rio shrugged. 'And it's safe to say Ernest Metcalfe was the attacker.' Rio shrugged again. 'You're not denying it was him now?'

'I'm not pressing charges and that's the end of it.' Wendy came down the stairs and sat next to him. She looked at him as if he was a toddler. 'Don't look at me as if I'm retarded. Why have you let him in, anyway?'

'He might get on my nerves most of the time, but he's your dad, and he's worried about you,' Wendy said. She looked at Jimmy. 'Tell him what's happening, Jimmy.'

'What's happening?' Rio asked, confused. 'What do you mean, what's happening?'

'Tell him, Jimmy,' Wendy insisted. 'It's important.'

'Tell me what, Jimmy?' Rio said sarcastically.

'People are angry about what happened to you,' Jimmy said. 'And they think Ernest Metcalfe assaulted you.' Rio shrugged that he didn't understand. 'My friends want to sort him out,' Jimmy added. 'They're going to hurt him.'

'Who is?' Rio asked. His eyes were bright now, suddenly interested in the conversation.

'It doesn't matter who they are,' Jimmy said. 'It's best you don't know.'

'I bet it's Conor and Wills,' Rio said. 'You're always with them. Pissheads all three of you,' he added. 'What are they gonna do, spill a pint on him?'

'Don't underestimate them, Rio,' Jimmy said, trying to stay calm, despite the slight. 'No one messes with Conor.'

'Your dad's right. Conor's a nutcase,' Wendy said. 'And a big nutcase at that. And Wills has had his moments too over the years. He's talking about hurting this pervert, which is fine by me, but only if he's actually done it?'

Rio bit his fingernails and looked from one parent to the other. His eyes darted about as if he was frightened to say what he was thinking but it was obvious his mind was ticking over at full speed.

'Listen, son,' Jimmy said, reaching out to touch Rio's hand. Rio pulled it away. 'You said you're not pressing charges?'

'That's up to me.'

'Not pressing charges is very different to saying you identified the wrong man,' Jimmy said. 'Those statements are poles apart.' Rio glared at him. Wendy looked impressed by what Jimmy had said. 'You told the police it wasn't Metcalfe, and that you got it wrong this morning.'

'So what?' Rio muttered. 'It's up to me.'

'But you said you're not pressing charges, which says to me that Metcalfe did attack you, but you're scared of him?' Jimmy said. Rio frowned and shrugged. He bit his lip and held back the tears. 'There's a huge difference between the two statements, son.' A tear ran down Rio's cheek. He screwed up his eyes and blushed red. 'Okay, you're scared. I get that,' Jimmy said. 'What happened between me leaving the hospital and you changing your mind?'

'I can't say,' Rio muttered.

'Did the police dissuade you from pressing charges?' Jimmy asked.

'No,' Rio said, sobbing openly now. 'I can't say anything. Just leave it alone. Let's forget it ever happened.'

'If it wasn't the police, and it wasn't us, it must be Metcalfe who frightened you off?' Jimmy said, looking into his son's eyes. Rio looked like he wanted to speak but dare not. 'If you don't feel like you can tell us, you can just nod if you want to?' Rio shook his head. Saliva dripped from his chin, and he wiped it away. 'Come on. Tell us the truth.'

'I've never seen him like this,' Wendy said, shaking her head. 'I'll kill that bastard. Look what he's doing to our son,' she added.

'Did Metcalfe get to you?' Jimmy asked. Rio screwed his eyes up and nodded. 'He did?' Another nod confirmed it. 'At the hospital?' Another nod. Jimmy took a deep breath. 'He threatened you while you were in the hospital and that's why you changed your story?' Another nod. Rio grabbed his mother and hugged her… the sobs unstoppable now. 'What a sneaky bastard. I'll kill him.'

'It's okay, son,' Wendy said. She looked over Rio's shoulder at Jimmy. Rio was shaking as he cried. 'You tell Conor to hurt that fucker. Tell him to do whatever he wants to do and more.' She stopped and looked at Rio. 'How did the bastard threaten you?' she asked. 'I was with you the entire time.' Rio sobbed uncontrollably. 'Except when you went to the toilets?' Rio nodded but didn't answer. 'It's the only time he was out of my sight. He must have come to the hospital looking for him. What kind of psycho does something like that?'

'He must have waited for him to go into the loos and then followed him,' Jimmy said, shaking his head.

'He's got some nerve to do that,' Wendy said.

'Are you fucking kidding me?' His jaw dropped open, and he snorted. 'How did he get in unnoticed and reach the first floor of the hospital and speak to Rio alone for long enough to cause this reaction?'

'He's crossed so many lines, I don't know where to begin,' Wendy said, flabbergasted. 'He clearly has no fear of being caught. The way he attacked Rio at the school and now this. He's a fucking psycho!'

'He's more than that, Wendy,' Jimmy said, contemplating what had happened. 'He's unbalanced.'

'What do you mean?' Wendy asked.

'Normal blokes wouldn't risk going into the hospital to threaten someone unless they were confident they could pull it off,' Jimmy said. 'This bloke is a different level of crazy and that worries me.' Wendy looked confused as she thought about what he was saying. 'I've heard he's ex-army, but even so, he seems to have no fear of being caught.' Jimmy shrugged. 'I mean, how is he even free to walk into the hospital?' Wendy didn't answer. 'Why wasn't he arrested straight away?'

'What are you saying?' Wendy asked.

'I'm saying this bloke is a sneaky fucker and we need to be very careful what we do next,' Jimmy said. 'Did he threaten to hurt you if you didn't drop the charges?' Rio shook his head. 'What did he say?'

'He said he would kill you and Mum, and no one would ever know he'd done it.' Rio sobbed. 'He stuck his finger so far up my nose I thought it was going to penetrate my brain.'

'He stuck his finger up your nose?' Wendy asked, astounded.

'Yes, right up. All the time he was whispering nasty shit in my ear. It's already broken. I've never felt pain like it,' Rio sniffled. 'I'm not pressing charges. He's a madman. I'm scared of him, Dad.'

'You don't need to be scared of him,' Jimmy said.

'Well, you didn't hear what he was saying about what he would do to Mum or see the look in his eyes,' Rio said, sniffling. 'I am scared of him and so should you be.'

****

Ernie knocked on the bedroom door and walked in without waiting for an answer. It was his house, and Helen was his child. He didn't need permission to enter her room. His blood was pumping through his body at an accelerated rate. As soon as she'd realised her accounts were deleted, she thought her devices were faulty, or the internet was down. Ernie told her what he'd done, and she was both confused and enraged. He said he'd explain things to her later, in private, but she'd stormed to her bedroom in floods of tears, swearing beneath her breath. Swearing in the house was not tolerated. It was the reaction he'd expected, but still, her use of foul language riled him. His temper was fraying. It was all he could do not to explode. He was so torn up with emotions. His insides felt like they were being twisted by an invisible claw.

Rio: *Have you kissed anyone with your mouth open?*

Slut: *No, but I want to x*

Rio: *I could teach you x*

Slut: *I'd like that x*

The messages were burnt into his brain and he felt too many extreme emotions to mention. Fear, disappointment, anger, definitely but the feeling of betrayal was overwhelming all others. He felt like his daughter hadn't just disappointed him, but had betrayed everything he believed in. Everything he'd tried to teach her, dignity, self-respect, pride, and honour had been discarded and shat all over in the blink of an eye. Helen reminded him of Naomi every time he looked at her, and this business with the Woods boy had scratched the scab off an old wound. A wound which went deep. It felt like a gaping hole in his very being. She was just like her mother; just the fucking same. Exactly the fucking same, the little slut.

Helen was sitting at her desk typing her homework, a well-used tissue scrunched in her left hand. She didn't look at him when he walked in, which was rude. Her impertinence was staggering. She was the one to blame here. All the Woods boy wanted was to fuck her. Didn't she realise that? All he was doing was making sure his thirteen-year-old girl wasn't fucked by anyone. Was he being unreasonable? Not a fucking chance was Woods being allowed to stalk his child. She was still a child, for fuck's sake. Ernie paused and took a breath before closing the door behind him.

'I know you're angry and upset with me, but I'm doing this for your benefit, not mine,' Ernie said. It felt like a lie because it was all for his own benefit, not Helen's but his reasoning was right and proper. She was a child. Slut.

'Whatever,' Helen muttered without turning around. 'I don't even know what I'm supposed to have done.'

'Really?' Ernie said. 'I suggest you have a think about it.'

'I'm not a fucking mind reader,' Helen muttered.

'I beg your pardon?' Ernie said, nearly choking. She'd never used that word in front of him before.

'I don't know what you think I've done wrong, but whatever it is, you've massively overreacted, as usual.'

'Oh, I've overreacted, have I?' Ernie said. 'Thank you for that, thirteen-year-old child of mine. I'm the adult in this house and as such, I'll make the decisions as to how I react to anything.'

'Whatever.'

'Don't be insolent.'

'I'm not being insolent on purpose. I'm not being anything at all. I'm upset because you've cut me off from all my friends and I don't know why.'

'I think you probably do, if you're honest with yourself,' Ernie said. 'And look at me when I'm talking to you.'

'I'm doing my homework, if that's all right with you?' Helen said. 'Or taking my laptop off me too?'

'I haven't taken anything from you, Helen,' Ernie said, simmering beneath the surface. 'You still have your phone, and you still have your laptop. I've disabled your social media profiles for your own good.'

'Oh my God,' Helen said, shaking her head. 'Do you have any idea what my friends will say when they realise I've been banned from social media?'

'You can still text them,' Ernie said.

'No one sends text messages, Dad,' Helen said. 'They cost money. We use social media so we can all talk together. All my friends will be disgusted with what you've done.'

'They will be "disgusted" with what I have done?'

'Yes. Disgusted. You're punishing me,' Helen said. 'Punishment doesn't work. Communication is the new smacking, but I wouldn't expect you to get that. My friends would be mortified if their dad did this to them,' Helen said. 'It's so embarrassing. I can't believe you've done that. I'm absolutely mortified.' Helen sniffled. 'I'll be the laughingstock of the entire school.'

'I'm not concerned about what your friends think.'

'Obviously. You're such a fucking dinosaur,' Helen muttered beneath her breath. 'I've never been so embarrassed in all my life.'

'What did you just say to me?' Ernie asked, shocked and angered.

'Just leave me alone,' Helen said. 'I don't want to discuss it with you.'

'"You don't want to discuss it"?' Ernie was flabbergasted. He couldn't work out when his child turned into a little person with an opinion. An opinion that was different to his own. 'Listen to me, young lady,' he said, biting his tongue. 'I decide what we discuss in this house, and I'll decide when we discuss it too and right now, you're sailing very close to the wind.'

'"Sailing close to the wind". What does that even mean?' Helen said, turning to face him. 'I've never been sailing in my life, so what the fuck are you talking about?'

'Do not use the f-word to me!' Ernie shouted. His face was reddening with anger. 'I am your father, and you will listen to me and talk to me with respect.' Spittle flew from his lips.

'OMG, he's shouting at me now. What century are we in?' she asked the room. 'That's bullying and no one bullies their children anymore,' Helen said, shaking her head. 'You're losing your grip, Dad.'

'I'm not losing my grip at all,' Ernie snapped. 'And I don't need a parenting assessment from you, young lady!'

'Really?' Helen said, putting down her pen. 'I get home from school and all my social media accounts have been deleted so I can't talk to my mates. We've had no conversations about it. I don't know why you've done it, and now you're in my room, shouting at the top of your voice and your face is so red it looks like it's going to explode,' she added. 'You're trying to bully and intimidate me, and I won't stand for it.'

'"You won't stand for it"?' he repeated. Ernie was stunned.

'No. Not for one minute. This is twenty-twenty-two where people communicate and discuss issues and reach compromises.'

'I don't believe I'm hearing this,' Ernie said, shaking his head. 'Who's been filling your stupid head with this nonsense?'

'Oh, so now I'm stupid as well,' Helen said. 'I guess I inherited that from you, then?'

'You need to be very careful,' Ernie warned.

'You should leave my space and come back when you can hold a conversation without spitting at me,' Helen said, sounding like a stranger. 'I'm just trying to finish my homework and you look like you're going to have a heart attack. I can't even ask anyone about this shitty assignment I have to hand in in the morning and I haven't got a scooby what the fuck I'm supposed to have done because you're being a dick…'

Ernie stepped forward and slapped her with the back of his hand with considerable force. Helen fell off her chair and banged her face on the desk leg. She landed on the floor in a heap. Blood trickled from a small gash on her cheek. She touched it and saw the blood on her fingers. Stars went off in her brain. She could taste blood in her mouth. Ernie stood over her and tried to control the red mist. His fists were clenched now.

'Nain! Nain!' Helen screamed for her grandmother. 'Help me!'

'Shut up!' Ernie snapped back to reality. 'Shut up!'

'I will not shut up!' Helen said.

'Be quiet!' Ernie tried to hush her.

'Fuck you.'

'That's enough!'

'You can't hit me. I'm calling the police.'

'Shut up!' Ernie shouted. 'Get in the bathroom and wash your face.'

'Not a chance. I want the police to see the blood.'

'You'll do as you're told, you little slut…'

'What on Earth is going on in here?' Rose said from the doorway.

'He's hit me, Nain.' Helen ran to her and hugged her, hiding behind her.

'What have you done?' she asked Ernie when she saw the blood on her cheek. It was also coming from the corner of her mouth. 'Oh, Ernie, what on Earth were you thinking?'

'He hit me. My mouth's cut inside,' Helen cried. 'I'm calling the police.'

'Be quiet,' Ernie shouted again.

'I will not,' Helen said. 'He just called me a slut. What father calls his daughter a slut?'

'Calm down,' Rose said. 'Both of you, please calm down.'

'I won't,' Helen said. Her lips were swelling. 'He will never hit me again.'

Ernie stormed out of the room and slammed the door behind him. He stomped down the stairs. The front door was opened and slammed closed a second later. Rose held Helen and let her breathing settle. She heard the Jeep starting and drive away.

'What happened, Helen?' Rose asked.

'Dad deleted all my social media accounts,' Helen said.

'Why?'

'I don't know. We argued, and he slapped me across the face. I want the police called and I'm pressing charges. No one has the right to hit me, not even my father.'

'He doesn't have the right to hit you, darling,' Rose said. 'We'll sort out that bruise on your face and stop your mouth bleeding first.'

'No,' Helen said. 'I'm reporting it. Mum always told me Dad had a bad temper and not to annoy him. I don't feel well,' she moaned. Her skin was grey.

'If you call the police, it will open a door, and if you open that door, Helen,' Rose said calmly. 'You can never close it. Social services will be involved, and your father will probably be charged with assault, which would mean you three wouldn't be allowed to live with him anymore.' Helen sniffled and shook her head. Rose could see her pupils were dilated. She was sinking. 'He's made a terrible mistake, but surely you don't want to be removed from his care?'

'What if he does it again or hits Hannah or Hilary?' Helen was becoming weaker.

'I'll speak to him and make sure nothing like this happens again.' Rose touched her cheek. It was swelling like a balloon. Rose saw it darkening and realised how bad it was. 'Good heavens,' she said. 'Let's get some ice on that.' The swelling was blackening as she looked at it. 'I think you may need to go to hospital. If we do, it will come out anyway. God help us.'

****

Bill Armstrong parked outside Kim's house. A solitary constable was standing on watch at the end of her drive. He was leaning against his patrol car, smoking a cigarette. Bill noticed an Audi parked across the street but didn't pay much attention. The lights were burning inside the house and a shadow moved across the bedroom window.

'Is someone in there?' Bill asked.

'Yes, sir,' the constable said, tossing his cigarette away quickly. 'Sorry about that. I wasn't expecting anyone else.'

'Don't worry about it. It was only arranged an hour ago,' Bill said. 'Who is in there?'

'Detective Superintendent Mann,' the constable said.

'Good. I'm here to meet her.'

'She's taking over the investigation, apparently.' He looked sheepish. 'That's what she told me, and it's too late to bother anyone to check. She did say she was meeting someone here, but she didn't say it was you.'

'Go and get yourself a brew and a burger from the drive-thru,' Bill said. 'We'll be here for a while.'

'Thanks, sir.'

Bill pushed open the front door and stepped inside. Olivia was coming down the stairs wearing a scene suit and overshoes. Her hair was smoothed into a ponytail and covered with a baseball cap. She smiled and lit up the room.

'Hello, Bill,' she said. 'It's nice to see a familiar face.'

'Thank you for taking this on,' Bill said. 'It's good to have you on-board. I asked for you in person but wasn't holding my breath that you would be released.'

'Released?' Olivia said, smiling. 'That makes me sound like a premiership player.'

'Released on loan to the conference league,' Bill said. 'I heard you were on an OCG case.'

'I was. The Eccles brothers,' Olivia said. 'We were literally about to sweep up the entire gang. The Eccles brothers were dumped on the moors this morning, minus their bits and pieces, so my current case came to a conclusion sooner than expected,' Olivia said. 'Plus, I was feeling a bit unappreciated when they asked me if I was interested, so here I am.'

'Whatever the reasons are, I'm glad you're here,' Bill said. 'Where are you staying?'

'I'm at the Travel Lodge tonight,' she said. 'I'll book somewhere expensive with a sea view tomorrow.'

'Good for you.' Bill smiled. 'Have you had a good look around?'

'I've walked the house, but I'm just putting things into perspective,' Olivia said. 'How's Alan Williams?'

'No change. He's out of surgery and still breathing, but he's been resuscitated several times already,' Bill said.

'Shotgun wounds will do that,' Olivia said. 'Not many people survive them.'

'He's a tough nut,' Bill said. 'We'll have to wait and see. What are your first impressions of the scene?'

'There's a lot of blood, which has been partially cleaned up for one reason or another and from what I read in the case files, Brandon Tanner, the man who built the booby trap is dead?' she said, frowning. 'From a bullet to the head?'

'Yes.'

'But he also had an axe wound to the skull?'

'Yes. We think Kim may have defended herself,' Bill explained. 'We have his associates locked up, but they're just a couple of petty crooks who went down with Tanner for their parts in a property scam.'

'A million miles away from this.'

'Definitely. This level of violence is not their bag,' Bill said. 'One of them pissed his pants when we arrested him.'

'Hard core,' Olivia said, smiling.

'They're not hardened criminals like the boys in the big cities. I've interviewed enough bad guys to know one when I see one. We'll be letting them go tomorrow morning.'

'So, they're ruled out completely?'

'Yes.'

'And it was DNA which led you to Brandon Tanner?' Olivia asked.

'Yes. Hair and skin on the axe recovered from the garage.'

'And we have no communication from the kidnappers, no ransom demands and no signs of a body?'

'Nope.'

'What do you know about Tanner?' Olivia asked.

'He's spent twelve years inside, on and off, for a string of offences, mostly violent crimes in connection with low-level dealing. He's a bully who likes to throw his weight around when he knows there's no chance of retaliation, but he's not smart enough to make sure no one testifies. So, he has a bundle of assaults and a couple of section eighteens and a couple of badly operated fraud scams but nothing in this category.'

'What category are we in?' Olivia asked, frowning. 'I've not made my mind up yet.'

'The well-organised category,' Bill said. 'The kidnap may have been the bait to attract someone to walk into the booby trap or taking Kim may be the main goal and the shooting is just a bonus.'

'Or they wanted both.'

'We're in the dark about the motive,' Bill said, shaking his head. 'I'm all ears as to what you think.'

'I think the key to this is Tanner,' Olivia said. 'I've arranged to meet Pamela Stone at his farm in the morning and one of the DSs from Holyhead is coming too.'

'Which one?'

'Richard Lewis,' Olivia said. 'It's been a rush, but he has the most service and the best performance figures.'

'He's a good detective,' Bill said. He paused, thinking of his next words carefully. 'There's something you probably don't know yet,' Bill added. Olivia smiled thinly.

'Is this where you tell me Jet-Wash Jenny is going to be in charge of the investigation?'

'No,' Bill chuckled. 'I take it you're not a fan?'

'I'm not a fan of her negativity and bullshit management techniques,' Olivia said. 'Let's not waste time talking about her. What else do I need to know?'

'This afternoon there was a hit and run in Caernarfon,' Bill said. 'Are you aware that's where the courts are?'

'Yes. And the custody suites for the island have been moved there too,' Olivia said.

'That's right.'

'I'm familiar with the structure of NWP.' She thought about her next words. 'As familiar as I can be with a Google search and a few hours spent in the car on the way here.'

'To cut a long story short, a crown court judge and senior barrister were run down and killed this afternoon. They were hit by a van, which mounted the pavement. The vehicle didn't stop and we haven't found it yet.'

'So, it was clearly intentional?'

'We don't know yet.'

'If it's not connected, you're telling me this because what?'

'Because two of my senior detectives have been targeted by persons unknown and a judge and barrister have been killed on the same day. This could be connected,' Bill said, losing eye contact. There was no conviction in his expression.

'Could be?' Olivia said, shaking her head.

'The chief constable is keen to keep them separate from each other, especially in the press. You can imagine the scenarios they could come up with if they put two and two together and come up with five.'

'What if they come up with four?' Olivia asked. She yawned. There was a niggle at the back of her mind. 'If they think we're covering up a connection, the coverage will be much worse.'

'You've lost me,' Bill said.

'Oh, come on, Bill,' Olivia said, shaking her head. 'You know that's bullshit and so do I.' She gestured at the window and the twinkling lights beyond. 'This is Sleepsville. Fuck all happens here, and two huge incidents happen on the same day, one involving a crown court judge and a senior barrister, the other involves two senior detectives and you want me to pretend they're not connected?'

she said, shrugging. 'Who is so deluded they think the press won't have linked this already?'

'That would be the chief,' Bill said.

'Aah, I see.'

'You know how these things work. Timing is everything.'

'I can see why she wants it kept schtum, but the cat will be out of the bag by now, surely?' Olivia said. 'Am I supposed to pretend I walk around with my eyes closed?'

'No. You must run the investigation as you see fit. That's why you're here. No internal influences of politics,' Bill said, blushing. 'I'm making you aware of how the CC wants to manage the press reporting of it. It's best to be transparent from the start.'

'And how long does she think it will take for the connection to be made, regardless of how we manage the investigation?' Olivia asked. 'A day, maybe a day and a half?'

'Please just bear it in mind,' Bill said.

'Who's dealing with the hit and run?'

'Caernarfon CID,' Bill said.

'I want everything they have so far first thing in the morning, and I want to talk to SIO,' Olivia said. 'I'm not waiting for it to become obvious this is a related attack. That would be a huge mistake. As far as the press is concerned, the CC and her office can field all the enquiries. Nothing will come from me, but I'm going to assume this is part of the investigation until we can prove otherwise.'

'And that's why I asked for you,' Bill said.

Chapter 32

Rose was sitting in the relatives' room with Hannah and Hilary. They were confused and upset by what had happened to Helen. The doctor was talking to a social worker outside the room. Rose knew that presenting an injured child at A&E would alert other agencies and now the ball was rolling, it would be impossible to stop. She could hear them talking and so could the girls, and the conversation was difficult to hear, especially as it was about their father. They were tired and teary, but she'd had no choice but to put them into the car, so she could get Helen to casualty. The left side of her face was like a football, her eye completely closed. She'd tried ringing Ernie, but his phone was going straight to voicemail. Rose was well aware that life as they knew it was about to change forever. There was no going back from this. The door opened and a pretty young woman walked in and smiled. She was wearing a long bubble jacket, which went down to her ankles, and she was clutching a laptop bag. Her long brown hair was messy, as if she'd been dragged from her bed in a hurry.

'I'm Emma Littler from the EDT at Anglesey Social Services,' she said. Rose looked confused. 'That's the emergency duty team,' she explained. 'We deal with all out of hours incidents.' She looked serious. 'I've been called out by the doctor in casualty because of a nonaccidental injury to Helen Metcalfe.'

'Oh dear,' Rose said. 'I'm sorry you have had to come out to deal with this. This is such a mess.'

'This is my job. Are you Helen's paternal grandmother?' Emma asked.

'Yes. I'm Rose. Ernest is my son.'

'Ernest struck Helen earlier on?' Emma asked. Rose nodded and filled up with tears. 'Did you witness him striking her?'

'No,' Rose said. 'I entered the room just after it happened.'

'What made you do that?' Emma asked.

'Helen was calling for me.'

'Calling?'

'Well, more like shouting.' Rose felt guilty, as if she was betraying her son.

'Was she shouting for help?'

'Yes.'

'He has given her one hell of a crack,' Emma said, lowering her voice. 'Her X-rays show that her cheekbone is fractured, and she's showing symptoms of concussion. I know he's your son, but he's committed a serious assault. You understand the severity of her injuries?'

'Yes, the doctor told me before you arrived,' Rose said, sniffling. 'He's a good dad. This is so out of character.'

'This is a section forty-seven assault, Rose, and it's very serious,' Emma explained. 'Do you know where Ernest is now?'

'No. He left straight away,' Rose said. 'He was so upset by what he'd done.'

'I'm sure he was,' Emma said. 'The police will be here soon. They'll need a statement from you and Helen before we can release you. Is there anywhere you can take the girls where Ernest won't be?'

'Yes. I have my own house nearby,' Rose said.

'Okay. That's good.'

'What will happen to him?'

'He'll be arrested and charged with a section forty-seven assault, and he'll be interviewed and then released on bail conditions. We will stipulate that he can't approach you or the girls.'

'He won't be able to see the girls?'

'No. Absolutely not. At the moment, he's deemed as a risk to all of them. We'll arrange contact once we've investigated thoroughly but contact in these cases is usually supervised in a specialised centre,' Emma explained. 'It's for the children's safety, of course.'

'I want to see my dad,' Hannah said tearily.

'So do I,' Hilary added. 'Where is he?'

'I don't know,' Rose said. 'But wherever he is, he's in trouble.'

Chapter 33

The Next Day

Kim had no idea if it was night or day. She'd drifted in and out of a troubled unconsciousness, neither asleep nor awake but desperately needing both. She was exhausted, frightened, hungry, thirsty, and in fear for her life. Her survival instincts told her to stay awake, but her brain and body were exhausted and needed rest. Periodically, her eyes would open and consciousness would reign momentarily and she would realise where she was. Panic would sweep over her, and she'd thrash against the restraints and try to shake the mask off, but to no avail. The harsh reality descended on her like a ton of bricks again and again. There was no way out of this hellhole without human intervention, and that was extremely unlikely. She was shackled to a trolley somewhere below ground, and no one could hear her scream. It reminded her of a film from the distant past. In space, no one can hear you scream. It was the tagline in the first *Alien* film from the late seventies before she was born and it had scared the shit out of her the first time she'd watched it. Yet she was more frightened now than any film could make her. A hundred times more frightened than she had ever been. She might as well be in space. Her predicament was worse than dire. It was tragic. The mask was suffocating and driving her demented. She needed it off so she could breathe freely. If she had to die, she wanted to die without the choking mask on. It was like being buried alive.

Kim knew she would die in that place and she knew death would be slow and agonising. Hunger and thirst would be her only companions until her organs began to shut down, then pain would engulf everything else. From her experience of seeing death many times and reading reports and autopsies, the process of events was well documented in her mind. She knew how it would go and there was nothing she could do to stop it. The voices in her head would criticise how she'd lived her life as death crept closer. If she hadn't chosen to become a police officer, none of this would have happened. If she'd married Stuart Atley as her mother wanted her to, she'd be living in Dubai as a kept housewife, lunching with friends, and bringing up his ginger kids. He was the most ginger person she'd ever met, so his kids would definitely be ginger. His skin was so pale, it was almost translucent, and his ginger pubes freaked her out. They were the reason she'd dumped him. She had to close her eyes when he wanted oral sex. It was the only way she could perform, and that wasn't the basis for a long and happy marriage.

Praying wasn't her thing, but she was praying now; praying death would come swiftly and end her torment. She was desperately trying to put time into context, but in the darkness, there was nothing to measure it by. It was hours before she'd come around enough to realise she was still holding the biro Pighead had given to her when she was being questioned. Her hand was clenched so tightly, the circulation was cut off and her fingers were numb, but when it dawned on her that she was holding the pen it was like an epiphany. She took the pen from her right hand and opened her fingers, allowing the blood to circulate. Pins and needles spread along her arm to her hand as the blood flowed to her extremities again.

When the numbness had dissipated, she felt the pen with both hands. It was the type which unscrews in the middle, has a clip on the outside, a spring inside, and an inner plastic tube that contains the ink, and a metal tip. She needed to know what they'd restrained her with to evaluate if the pen and its parts might be of value unlocking them. Her right hand held the pen, while her left felt for the opposite wrist. They were handcuffs, but not the rigid ones she used at work. These were older models with a steel chain between each cuff; the type they used to use when she first joined the force. Kim had seen them picked dozens of times and had done it herself on a few occasions. That had been at work, when she was in uniform, bored on patrol. She remembered her partner making a bobby-pin from a paperclip and showing her how it was done. It had taken her forty minutes to tip the lock in the right direction and she could see what she was doing at the time.

Now, she was blinded by the mask and all she had at her disposal was the pen. She thought she heard a dull thud. A draft touched her neck, or was she hallucinating?

She needed to get the cuffs off if she was to live. Jason Bourne would be out of them in seconds, unfortunately, this was not Netflix.

This was real life and death, her life and her death.

She wasn't sure if she could make a bobby-pin from the spring. The rest was hard plastic and no use in the lock-picking game. Plastic was brittle and could snap and if it snapped in the lock, she was as good as dead. She held the pen in both hands and debated unscrewing it when she heard a key in the door lock. Then she heard the sound of the door opening and the light switch being flicked on, although it was muffled. Her heart pounded against her chest.

Boom, boom, boom.

Had someone come to rescue her?

'Hello again,' a voice said. Her heart froze and her breath stuck in her lungs. It was him. 'Everyone else has gone but I couldn't leave without saying goodbye. We've got unfinished business and there's no one to disturb us this time.'

CHAPTER 34

Olivia Mann suited up and went across the muddy yard towards the Tanner farmhouse. The stars were twinkling over Holyhead Mountain, and she could see the beam from the lighthouse momentarily illuminating the lower slopes. DS Lewis was waiting for her with Pamela Stone. It was early in the morning and still dark, but the first members of the dawn chorus were tweeting tentatively. As she approached the doorway, the light from inside the house touched her features. Richard was taken aback. The new gaffer was absolutely stunning. He scratched the stubble on his face and wished he'd shaved, breathing in his beer belly as far as it would go, which wasn't far.

'Close your mouth,' Pamela whispered in his ear as the superintendent approached. 'You look simple.'

'What?' Richard stammered. Pamela nudged him.

'Close your mouth and stop breathing in, you'll suffocate.'

'I'm not breathing in,' Richard protested. He blushed and sucked in harder.

'DS Lewis?' Olivia asked.

'That would be me,' Richard said, nodding. 'It's a pleasure to have you here,' he added. 'Welcome to Anglesey.'

'Thank you for turning out so early in the morning but I need to catch-up before the briefing later,' Olivia said.

'No problem,' Richard said, smiling too wide.

She turned to Pamela. 'Thank you for meeting me at this ungodly hour, Pamela. Much appreciated.'

'Not a problem,' Pamela said. 'What have you done to be sent from the big city to this outpost?'

'I think I murdered a nun in a previous life,' Olivia said. Richard thought about protesting but wanted to make a good impression. 'Although, I did have a choice in the matter believe it or not.' Richard looked surprised. 'Don't look so surprised. I chose to be here. It's a long story.' Olivia nodded towards the hallway. 'Shall we get on with it. I want to find our missing DI and so far, I haven't heard anything that makes sense.'

'Where do you want to start?' Richard asked. He turned and walked down the hallway to the living room door. 'Tanner was found in here,' he said, gesturing with his hand. Pamela showed her an image of the body on her tablet. 'He had a revolver in his right hand and the contents of his skull were up the wall.' He rolled his eyes. 'They still are, actually. A bit crusty now though.'

'What type of gun was it?' Olivia asked.

'Good question,' Richard said, nodding his approval of her thought process. Olivia hid a smile and Pamela rolled her eyes skyward. 'It was a Webley Revolver.'

'It's an old model,' Pamela said, showing her an image.

'That's the Mark 6,' Olivia said. Her companions looked impressed. 'The British Army used it as their service revolver from nineteen-fifteen until nineteen-thirty-two.' Pamela and Richard looked at each other, impressed. 'It's a forty-five calibre, six-shooter, phased out of service in the early thirties.'

'Really?' Richard muttered, staring into her eyes. They seemed to sparkle but were deep and intelligent. 'The early thirties, you say. Fascinating.'

'Yes. It was replaced by the thirty-eight Smith and Wesson, which was more reliable, cheaper, and lighter to carry.' Richard opened his mouth again but didn't speak. Pamela smiled and nodded. 'I studied firearms during my degree,' she explained. 'My dissertation was on British Army weaponry.'

'Interesting,' Richard said, eyebrows raised.

'The established OCGs are using nine millimetres nowadays, mostly Glocks. This is an antique.'

'Meaning what?' Richard asked.

'Meaning Tanner didn't have access to an OCG arsenal, or he wouldn't be carrying this weapon. Nine millimetres are so much more glamourous. I blame Netflix.'

'And we have to assume it's his?' Richard asked.

'Not necessarily,' Olivia said. 'We just need to be mindful that this weapon is rare. There aren't many of these around and most of the ones which turn up are found in Ireland,' Olivia said, swiping through the images of the body.

'Ireland?' Richard asked. 'Why do you think that is?'

'Because the last place they saw service was Northern Ireland, and a lot of them never found their way home when the army stopped using them. Most of them would have stayed with whoever had been allocated them. I doubt there was a formal collection of existing service revolvers when the new one was rolled out. It's not beyond reasonable doubt to accept some of them found their way here, which is a ferry ride away, right?'

'They would be easy enough to smuggle across, especially in the thirties,' Richard said. 'I've heard many stories about trawlermen buying weapons as souvenirs when they were in distant ports. Some of the old pubs used to have them on the walls as decorations.'

'That's where most of them end up,' Olivia said, nodding. 'Private collections and antique shops were full of them in the seventies until people realised they were still functional firearms.' She paused for thought. 'The good thing about revolvers is the amount of GSR they expel during firing. Have we had GSR results back yet?'

'Not yet,' Pamela said, 'but I made it a priority.'

'It has to be,' Olivia said. 'We need to know if he pulled the trigger.'

'You think it might not be suicide?' Richard asked, frowning.

'I'm exploring the evidence, Sergeant,' Olivia answered. She pointed to the image of Tanner. 'This is an axe wound on his head and the axe was left at the scene of Kim's abduction?'

'Yes,' Pamela said. 'It was Kim's axe, we think. She had a log burner and there's a stack of wood next to the garage.'

'And the skin and hair on the blade were visible to the naked eye?'

'Yes,' Pamela said. 'Although it was found underneath her vehicle behind a wheel.'

'There was an attempt to clean up the rest of the scene at Kim's house,' Olivia said. 'I had a look around late last night and things don't add up.' She frowned.

'In a fashion,' Pamela said, showing her the bloodstains from the staircase. 'There were blood trails up the stairs, which had been treated with water and scrubbed with bedding and towels. We found them in the washing machine.'

'How badly would this axe wound have affected him?' Olivia asked. 'I mean, could he have walked, talked, put a gun to his own head, and pulled the trigger?'

'It's possible,' Pamela said. 'But not probable.'

'So, let's add all that up. The axe belonged to Kim and was in the garage?'

'Yes, under the car.'

'But there was no blood on the floor?'

'There was spatter but no pooling,' Pamela said.

'If he was hit with a single axe blow, hard enough to split his skull and penetrate an inch and a half, he would have gone down, surely?' Olivia asked herself aloud. 'There would be pooling on the garage floor.'

'Maybe he fell against the car and stayed on his feet,' Richard said. 'Or maybe one of his associates helped him.'

'Or maybe he was hit somewhere else,' Olivia said. 'Somewhere where there was more blood.'

'Like the stairs?' Richard asked.

'Or the bedroom, where the booby trap was placed,' Olivia said.

'That would make sense,' Pamela said. 'But it would be unlikely the axe found its way under the car by itself. It didn't fall out of his skull in the garage.'

'What if Kim had it, ran upstairs to get away from her attackers and struck him with it in the bedroom?'

'As Pamela said, possible but not probable,' Olivia said, shaking her head. She walked into the kitchen. 'He was building more booby traps in here?'

'Three more,' Pamela said, showing her more images. 'Each one was the same as the one used to injure Alan.'

'We have to assume that if he built them, he installed the device too, so Tanner would have been in that bedroom and we know someone was injured in there because of the blood on the bedding and mattress,' Olivia said.

'I think that's a reasonable assumption,' Pamela agreed.

'What if Kim didn't hit him at all?' Olivia asked. 'What if someone else hit him with the axe and he staggered from the bedroom, along the landing and down the stairs?'

'And then whoever hit him tossed the axe under the car?' Richard asked.

'Yes,' Olivia said.

'Why would they do that?' Richard asked. 'It was only a matter of time before we found it.'

'My point exactly,' Olivia said, nodding. Richard looked baffled. 'Why would he make four of the devices?' Olivia asked.

'Maybe he planned to attack more of us,' Richard said. 'But Kim whacked him and spoiled his plans.'

'Or someone else whacked him.'

'Why?'

'He was the fall guy,' Olivia said.

'Not a man on a mission?' Richard asked.

'I don't think so. If that was the case, we would have to assume he was making them for his own use?' Olivia said, shrugging. 'It would mean he had an agenda against Kim and Alan and maybe the wider force in general, but I doubt it.'

'Who else would he be making them for?' Richard asked.

'That's what we need to find out,' Olivia said. 'He could have been making them for money, commissioned by another party that we haven't identified yet. When we find out the answer to that question, we will know who took DI Davies and why. And if we can do that, we will find her.' She paused.

'You don't think he organised this, do you?' Richard asked. Olivia smiled and shrugged, not committing just yet. 'Me neither,' Richard added.

'That's reassuring,' Olivia said. 'Do we have his financials yet?'

'They should be with us this morning,' Richard said.

'From his records, this man is a low-level opportunist, drifting from one shit idea to the next, trying to make a quick buck without being arrested,' Olivia said, looking at Richard. 'You know the island. Is that a fair reflection?'

'If anything, you're gifting him with too much credit,' Richard said. 'He's certainly not masterminding the abduction of a police detective or the assassination of another. This is way beyond Tanner's skill set.'

'We're on the same page, Sergeant,' Olivia said.

'We are?' Richard said, pleased with himself.

'So, my gut feeling is Tanner doesn't do anything for nothing and there are no political or religious ideologies in play here, so…' Olivia left the sentence hanging for Richard.

'So, his motive is financial,' Richard said. 'Tanner's working for someone further up the chain.'

'Exactly,' Olivia said. 'And they threw him under the bus and sent us running in the wrong direction.'

'The axe with DNA on it was too easy to find?' Pamela agreed, nodding.

'They blurred all the lines with the partial clean up and then chucked us a bone to chew on to keep us occupied,' Olivia said. 'I want you to get on the telephone to whoever has those financials and find out where they are and when we'll have them.'

'Consider it done,' Richard said, taking out his phone. He walked out of the kitchen towards the front door and out of earshot while he worked out who to call at such an early hour. He decided

Chod might have a better idea and called him. It went straight to voicemail. 'For fuck's sake,' he muttered to himself. He decided to delegate and called the operations room.

'DC Thomas, Holyhead MIT.'

'Annie, it's Richard,' he said, lowering his voice. Annie was a detective from Caernarfon, drafted in at every opportunity because of her resourcefulness. She also had the gift of organisation. 'I'm with the new gaffer at the Tanner farm.'

'Ahh, when I heard your voice, I did wonder if you'd shit the bed,' Annie said. 'This is way too early for you.'

'You know me so well.'

'What's she like?'

'Sharp as a tack,' Richard said. 'I'm not easily impressed, but this lady knows what she's doing and some. She wants to focus on Tanner's financials. Who's sorting them out?'

'Me, as it happens,' Annie said. 'I'm expecting them to be with me as soon as the bank employees log on, which should be at seven o'clock.' She checked her watch. 'Fifty minutes from now.'

'What are you expecting to receive?'

'Two personal accounts, an online business account with a company I've never heard of, and a limited company account, Tanner's registered as the only director.'

'Brilliant,' Richard said. 'I'll let her know. Thanks, Annie.'

'You're welcome,' Annie said. 'Don't be taking the credit for it.'

'As if I'd do that,' Richard said, chuckling. He ended the call. Olivia and Pamela were walking out of the front door. 'Tanner has multiple accounts and I've arranged for them to be sent to operations as soon as the bank logs on, which should be in about fifty-minutes,' he said with a straight face. 'DC Thomas from Caernarfon will get them in case we're still out of the station. She's a whizz with financials.'

'Well done, Richard,' Olivia said, walking towards her car. 'Thanks again for coming out so early. I'll see you back at the station.'

'No problem. I'm glad I could help.' Richard watched her climb into her vehicle and drive away down the muddy farm track.

'I think you've got a crush on her,' Pamela said, walking back to her van. She smiled over her shoulder. 'Proper smitten.'

'Nonsense. It's early days, but I think we have a mutual respect for each other.'

'Nope. You have a boss-crush going on.'

'Don't be ridiculous,' Richard said, blushing.

CHAPTER 35

Kim was frozen stiff with fear. She felt him approaching like a dark tornado on the horizon that would wreak havoc, death, and destruction when it arrived. An evil, irresistible force focused on her and her alone. She wanted to scream for help, but it wouldn't help her now. His footsteps approached. He was next to her, standing over her. She could sense him, hear him breathing, fast and shallow and worst of all, she could smell him. Alcohol, cigarettes, and rank body odour. She felt his breath on her neck and tried to pull away.

'There's nowhere to go, silly,' he whispered. There was a slur in his speech. 'Don't play hard to get.' He was drunk. Kim froze. 'I know you can hear me in there,' he whispered. 'Are you scared?' he chuckled dryly. 'You should be.' He put his hand on her right breast and squeezed hard. 'Nice tits,' he said, searching for her nipple. He found it and twisted it between finger and thumb. 'Do you like that?'

'Get your hands off me, you bastard!' Kim hissed. She kicked and bucked at the restraints, but they wouldn't give. 'Don't touch me!'

'Or what?' he asked calmly. 'Will you shout louder and struggle harder?' He moved his right hand between her legs and rubbed hard at the material of the jumpsuit. 'Go on, struggle. Scream and shout all you like because nothing is going to stop me doing whatever I want.'

'Please stop it!'

'I'm only just getting started,' he said. 'Once we get going, you'll get into it. And if you don't, who cares anyway?'

'Please, just let me go,' Kim sobbed. 'I want to go home.'

'Oh, dear,' he said. 'You're never going home, lovely. And I wish I could tell you we're going to have fun before you die but you won't. You're going to wish you were dead a long time before it happens so, you'll just have to embrace the experience.' He laughed. 'I know I will. Every second.'

Chapter 36

When Helen woke up, there were two uniformed officers standing next to her bed and a brass band was marching through her head. One eye was virtually closed, and the side of her face was swollen so badly, the skin felt tight and throbbed painfully. Her mouth was dry as a bone and she had the coppery taste of blood on her tongue. Nainy Rose was hovering next to the bed, looking worried, tired, and weary.

'Here you are,' she said, putting a cup to her lips. 'Take a sip of water and I'll call the nurse.' Helen sipped and sat up a little. The memories of what happened returned quickly. She started to cry. 'Don't get upset,' Rose said. A nurse appeared and checked her pulse.

'How are you feeling?' she asked.

'Sore and my head aches,' Helen said. The nurse handed her two painkillers and a cup of water. 'Is my dad here?' Helen asked.

'No, and if he was, I would have a few choice words to say to him,' the nurse said curtly. She turned to the police officers. 'Five minutes and no longer,' she said, walking away.

'What's happened to Dad?' Helen sniffled. 'Has he been arrested?'

'No, not yet, but he will be when we find him,' Bob said. 'I'm Sergeant Dewhurst and this is Sergeant Byfelt. We just need to ask you a few questions, okay?'

'Okay,' Helen nodded. 'Will he go to jail?'

'That's not up to us and it's not for you to worry about right now. The injuries to your face look like they were caused by a punch?' Bob asked.

'Yes. But not a fist.'

'So, not a punch?'

'He slapped me with the back of his hand, and I fell off my chair and banged my face on the desk, I think,' Helen said, sniffling. 'Can I see my face?' she asked Rose.

'Maybe later, when the police have finished their questions,' Rose said. 'You're not looking your best at the moment. It might be a bit if a shock, but these things always look worse than they are.'

'Worse than they are? I'm not sure it could be worse. She has a broken cheekbone,' Bob said, shaking his head. 'I did a bit of boxing when I was younger, but I never looked like that.'

'That's not helpful,' April said, interrupting. 'Bruising always looks nasty.'

'I'm just saying she has a broken cheekbone,' Bob said. 'It's not something that goes unnoticed.'

'I'm aware of that,' Rose said curtly. 'I wasn't trying to make light of it.'

'Good,' Bob said. 'It would be a mistake to play this down to anything less than what it is.'

'And what would that be?' Rose asked.

'A serious assault on a minor.'

'Why did your dad hit you?' April asked, changing the subject.

'I'm not sure, exactly.'

'try to explain what actually happened to me in your own words,' April coaxed. 'Let's start with what happened when you got home.'

'We went for tea at Langdons first, then when I got home, I went to talk to my friends online, but he'd deleted all my social media accounts,' Helen said. 'I thought my tablet was broken at first, but everything was working except my social media.'

'He hadn't told you what he had done at that stage?'

'No. He hadn't told me anything. He just deleted them while I was at school.'

'Okay, so you find out your accounts have been deleted. Then what happened?'

'I was upset, so I went to my room to do my homework. He came into my room and told me it was for my own good. I told him all my friends would be disgusted with what he'd done. That made him angry. We argued, and I swore at him and called him a dick. Then he hit me.'

'You shouldn't have called him that,' Rose said, thin lipped. 'No wonder he got angry.' She turned to the police officers. 'He doesn't tolerate bad language. His father was the same. I never heard him swear more than a couple of times in thirty-nine years of marriage.'

'Being called a dick is hardly what I would call a trigger to break his daughter's cheekbone,' Bob said.

'I'm sure that's not what he meant to happen,' Rose said.

'When a grown man hits a child, a considerable amount of damage can be expected,' Bob said. 'That's not rocket science.'

'I'm just saying it must have been in the heat of the moment,' Rose said.

'Ah, the old red mist defence,' Bob said, winking. Rose was going to argue, but decided not to bother. She was on a losing wicket. 'I'm curious as to why he deleted your social media accounts,' Bob said. Helen shrugged. 'That seems a little extreme. Why do you think he did that?'

'He didn't say,' Helen said. 'I didn't get the chance to find out.'

'Was it anything to do with Rio Woods?' Bob asked. The reaction on her face told him what he needed to know.

'Rio?' Helen whispered. Her mind was ticking over. Bob could hear the wheels clicking into place. 'Why would you mention him? How do you know Rio?' she asked.

'Rio was attacked yesterday on his way to school,' Bob said. Rose looked pale but didn't speak. 'He was badly injured during the attack, and he identified your father as his attacker.'

'OMG,' Helen whispered. 'He is so embarrassing.'

'Is that why you were at our house yesterday?' Rose asked. Bob nodded. 'Oh dear.' Rose looked confused. 'But he was at home in bed.'

'So, the question is, have you been chatting to Rio online?' Bob asked, ignoring Rose.

'Yes. Sort of. Just chatting,' Helen said, blushing.

'Was there any flirting going?' Bob asked.

'Good heavens,' Rose said. 'She's thirteen!'

'And that's my point,' Bob said, glancing at April with an I told you so look on his face. 'Was there any flirting?'

'A bit maybe,' Helen said. 'But Dad couldn't have known, could he?'

'There are apps which can monitor mobiles and social media accounts,' April said.

'OMG, he hacked me,' Helen said, shaking her head. 'What a weirdo.'

'It would explain a lot of things if he was monitoring your phone,' Bob said. 'You said your son was at home yesterday morning?' Bob said, looking at Rose.

'He was in bed with a bad back,' Rose said. 'He said goodbye to the girls when they went to school.'

'I can't believe Dad's hacked me and attacked Rio,' Helen said, crying. 'Everyone will know by now. Oh God, this is so embarrassing. No one will ever talk to me again. He's lost the plot completely.'

'Did you actually see your dad yesterday morning?' April asked, frowning.

'No,' Helen said. 'He always locks the door.'

'So, he said goodbye to you through the door?' Bob asked, nodding.

'Yes.'

The nurse came back in and gestured to the police officers that it was time to go.

'Okay,' Bob said. 'Our time is up. You get some rest, and we'll keep you posted.'

'Do you have any idea where he would go?' April asked Rose.

'No.' Rose shook her head. 'I haven't got a clue.'

CHAPTER 37

Kim heard the metallic click of a knife being opened and she groaned in despair, like a wounded animal in a trap. Her heart was pounding in her chest like never before; she felt like it was going to burst apart. He tugged at her jumpsuit, looking for the zip.

'Let's unwrap you, shall we?' he said jovially. His hand reached inside and squeezed her left breast hard. 'Like a big juicy chocolate orange. Tap it and unwrap it, remember that?'

'Get off me, you fucking freak!'

'That's not going to happen, so stop whining. Do you like to be bitten?' he asked, biting the skin at the base of her neck.

'Aah!' she cried out. 'Fuck off!'

'You do like it.' He laughed, doing it again.

'Okay, okay, stop!' Kim said, trying to keep her voice from cracking. 'Take this fucking mask off first and I'll do whatever you want.'

'What?'

'You heard me,' Kim said, catching her breath. 'Take the fucking thing off.'

'I'm not stupid,' he said but there was uncertainty in his voice.

'You want it all, don't you?' Kim said. 'Take this fucking thing off me before I choke to death. I'll do what you ask.'

'You'll see my face,' he muttered.

'And what?' Kim shouted. 'I'll be dead soon. Who am I going to describe you to?'

'That's a good point.'

'Take it off!'

She felt him reaching for the zip and tugging at the mask. It parted and fresh air rushed in. The light hurt her eyes, but the relief was overwhelming. She began to cry again. The mask fell away onto the trolley beneath her.

'Don't put that thing back on me,' Kim said, sniffling. 'Kill me first.' She blinked to focus on him. He was an overweight man in his fifties, balding on top with grey stubble on his chin. He didn't look frightening at all, a little pathetic if anything. 'Right, what's your name?'

'You can call me Des,' he said. He winked. She cringed inside. The sad fuck winked at me, she thought.

'Okay, Des, thanks for taking that off me,' Kim said. 'I need one more thing from you.' He looked confused. 'Unless you take me to the toilet out there, you're going to need rubber gloves and a gasmask to come anywhere near me.' Kim could see him mulling over his options. 'I'm minutes away from shitting myself and I haven't been able to go since you brought me here. I don't think either of us wants that to happen, do we?'

'I like to slip it up the backdoor whenever possible,' Des said, grinning. 'Better for both of us if we get you to the loo.' He stopped smiling.

'Nice to see romance isn't dead,' Kim said. 'I bet you're in demand wherever you go,' she muttered.

'I'll unfasten you from the trolley and walk you there, but if you put one foot wrong, I'll slash your throat and fuck you while you're dying, understand me?' Des warned.

'Perfectly,' Kim said. 'Come on, Des. You'd better hurry.'

'Don't push it,' Des said. 'I don't like being told what to do,' he added, unlocking the shackles which fastened her wrists and waist to the trolley. She moved her arms, and the blood began to circulate. Cramp spread through her limbs as he unfastened her ankles.

'I bet you do,' Kim said. Des frowned. 'I bet you love being told what to do under the right circumstances.'

'Is this where you try to get me to drop my guard while you look for an opportunity to run away?'

'Something like that,' Kim said.

'Don't bother,' Des said. 'I'm not stupid.'

'I'm struggling to hold it in here,' Kim said.

'Don't be disgusting,' Des said, frowning. 'Sit up,' Des said. Kim sat up and the room began spinning.

'You're going to slit my throat and fuck me while I'm dying, but I'm disgusting?'

'Talking about shit,' he said. 'Makes me want to retch. Stand up.'

'Give me a second,' she said. She blinked to focus her eyes. The dizziness settled. 'Okay. I can walk.'

'Swing your legs over the edge and stand up,' Des said. Kim did as she was asked. The blood was circulating, and her head was clearing. 'Walk with me,' he said, holding her by the elbow. Kim took tentative steps, scared of her legs giving way beneath her. 'That's it,' he added. 'You really are pretty,' he said. Kim felt like vomiting. 'Under different circumstances, I think we could have been an item.'

'The only circumstances that would happen is if I was dead.'

'That can be arranged easily,' Des said, squeezing her arm.

'That hurts!' Kim said.

'Good.'

They reached the door, and she stepped into the dank corridor. He was right behind her as they approached the toilet.

'What is this place, anyway?' Kim asked as they neared the doorway.

'It's a bunker,' Des said. 'We're a long way underground. If you run, you won't get far.'

'My legs and hands are fastened,' Kim said, holding out her wrists.

'I know.'

'I can't get out of this jumpsuit with these on,' she said. 'Unfasten them before I mess myself.' Des thought about it but couldn't come up with a way she could use the toilet with the jumpsuit in place. 'Hurry up, Des. I'm desperate here.'

'One wrong move,' Des said, holding up the blade in the dull light.

'And you'll slit my throat and fuck me anyway,' Kim said sarcastically. 'You said that already.' Des reluctantly took out the key and unfastened her wrists. 'Thank you.'

Kim rubbed at them and shuffled into the toilet. There was suspicion in his eyes as she pushed the door closed. She unfastened the jumpsuit and sat on the toilet. Her eyes scanned the walls, ceiling, and floor for something, anything that could help. It was a fruitless search, compounded by the lack of anything to wipe herself with. Her mind went back to a story Alan used to tell after a few whiskeys about a prisoner who made a run for it. She wasn't going to let that fat piece of shit violate her while she still had breath in her body. It was crunch time.

CHAPTER 38

Lisa Willis tried her ex-husband's number again for the tenth time. There was no answer. It was ringing out and clicking to voicemail, which was irritating because Wills had recorded his message as if he was answering the call. He said hello six times before laughing and saying he wasn't available to answer but to leave a message. No matter how many times she heard it, she said hello and then kicked herself when it wasn't him. It was instinct to say hello. Wills was a dick-head who thought he was funny, especially when he was pissed, which was always. That's why she was no longer Mrs Willis, because she couldn't endure his four-day benders, which would only end when he had no more money to spend. He would come home shattered, broke, and tearful, promising it was the last time and that he wouldn't do it again. It would take them weeks to pay off all his bar tabs and as soon as they were debt free, he would go on another bender. Prick. Divorced prick.

Lisa was frantic. She had a job interview on the railway, working as a steward on the trains, which was a great job, if you could get. Holyhead was short on quality employment opportunities and the railway was well paid and highly sought after. Wills had promised to look after their eight-year-old son for the morning and he promised to be at her house for ten o'clock, but it was already half past. Her interview was at eleven and there was no sign of him. The wanker. If it wasn't for sharing responsibility for their child, she would have nothing to do with him. He was a waster. She parked her car outside his house on Treseifion Estate and turned off the engine.

'Stay here,' she said to her son, Jon.

'Why can't I come to the door?' Jon complained. He loved going to his dad's because he could do all the stuff his mum didn't allow.

'Because your father is a complete toss-pot and I need to know if he's sober before you go anywhere, so do as you're told and stay there,' Lisa said, climbing out of the car. She marched up the path and banged on the door. It swung open and hit the wall with a thump.

'Wills?' she called, stepping inside. There was no answer, but there was a terrible smell. 'Why is the front door open, Wills?' she said, walking up the hallway. The kitchen was empty, but there was a wide red smear on the tiles. 'Are you pissed?' she shouted, staring at the red stains. It was blood, no doubt about it. 'You're supposed to be minding our son, you piss-head. I asked you to do one thing for me,' she shouted upstairs. Wills didn't answer. She noticed bloody finger marks on the walls, as if someone had been pulled down the hallway against their will. 'Wills?' Lisa shouted, frightened now. 'Are you all right?'

Lisa reached the living room door, which was closed. It was never closed. The handle was smeared with blood. She didn't want to open it, but knew she had to. 'Wills?' she called, knocking on the door. There was no reply. Lisa went back to the kitchen and grabbed a tea towel and used it to open the living room door and pushed it open. She screamed at the same time as Jon began to scream and she realised he'd followed her into the house. She put her hands over his eyes and picked him up, stumbling out of the house, but it didn't stop him screaming nor did it remove what he had seen from his mind.

CHAPTER 39

Conor Peterson woke up with a jolt. His car alarm was going off, which was worrying as it was garaged at the back of his house. He was paranoid about it. His unpopularity had resulted in dozens of attacks on his vehicle and vandalism to his home. Conor made more enemies than friends, and he'd paid the price over the years. It had been scratched more times than he could remember, long ones too, from the front wing all the way to the rear panels. They were always too deep to buff out, and he had to respray it each time, which had cost him dear. The tyres had been slashed on more than one occasion and his windscreen was smashed with a headstone from Maeshyfryd Cemetery, which was across the road from his house. That was the final straw, as they'd used his family's headstone. His mother, father, and both grandparents were in that plot, and the bastards desecrated it by removing the headstone and tossing it through his windscreen. He'd been so incensed, he trawled the streets of Holyhead for a full week, quizzing everyone who'd had a grudge against him as to their whereabouts. That was a long list with several offshoots of people related to those who didn't like him. Of course, nobody confessed, and nobody grassed but one of his arch-rivals reportedly went to

London the day after. That seemed to be an odd coincidence. That was when he had a garage built and a car alarm fitted to his old Land Rover. Nothing had happened for years until now.

Conor sprang out of bed, scratching his testicles as he peered through the curtains. He couldn't see anyone, but the garage door was open, and it had been padlocked, which meant only one thing. Someone had broken the lock off it. He pulled on a pair of shorts and stuffed his feet into his battered Adidas trainers. He grabbed a grey hoodie from the banister when he reached the bottom of the stairs and wrestled it on as he walked through the kitchen. He took the biggest carving knife he had from the block and unlocked the back door.

'I'm going to carve my name into your face, you fucker!' he shouted as he stepped onto the path. 'You'll be sorry, just you see if you're not.' A flash of steel flashed in front of his eyes, briefly before a shovel hit him square in the face.

CHAPTER 40

Kim took a deep breath and opened the toilet door nervously. Sure enough, Des was waiting directly outside, a leering expression on his face. He thought he was about to win the sexual lottery. His victim was in a weakened state and was being compliant. She'd said she would do as he asked. Happy days. His eyes were narrowed and beady, and he still held the knife in his right hand.

'Are you done, darling?' he asked, grinning.

'Darling?' Kim repeated, shaking her head. 'You've got a screw loose.'

'Let's get you back on your trolley, shall we?' he said. Kim hesitated. 'Come on. I'm gagging for it,' he snapped. 'Stop stalling.'

Kim stepped forward and aimed. She tossed the still warm turd like a dart player aiming for the bull's eye. It hit him in the middle of his face, splattering into his eyes. A lump broke free and hit him just below his nose and stuck for a second before sliding down into his open mouth. He was stunned for a moment while his brain tried to figure out what had happened, then he gagged as the smell hit him. The realisation that he had shit in his mouth sent him staggering blindly backwards, spitting and frothing like a man possessed.

'You dirty bitch!' Des shouted. He wiped at his mouth with the back of his sleeve, and rubbed his eyes, which made things considerably worse. He had a horrified expression on his face. 'I can't believe this. You'll be fucking sorry!'

The turd dropped to the floor and Kim picked it up and closed the gap between them. She slammed her hand into his face and smeared the excrement in his eyes and nose, grinding it in. He roared in anger and stabbed at her blindly, instinct driving his response. Kim felt the cold steel piercing her abdomen just above her left hip. The pain was debilitating, and she screamed out. She took the pen from her sleeve and jabbed it hard into his left eye. She heard his eyeball pop like someone squeezing bubble wrap. He screamed like a banshee and slashed at her. The blade cut through her ear, severing the lobe from her head. It opened a gash which ran from her ear across her throat to her collarbone. She felt blood running down her chest, hot and sticky. Des staggered backwards, stabbing again as he stumbled. The blade pierced her beneath the floating rib, and she felt her knees buckle, but she was desperate not to fall. She grabbed at the blade instinctively and held it tightly. He tried to pull it back, and the blade cut through her fingers. She stabbed him in his right eye with the pen. There was another audible pop. The scream sounded like something from the darkest pits of hell. His wail was ear-piercing as he collapsed in a writhing heap on the damp concrete, clutching his ruined eyes as blood and jelly-like aqueous humour trickled between his fingers.

Kim stepped back and rested against the wall, holding his knife now. Her breathing was coming in short gasps, and she was feeling faint. She looked at the knife in her hand, covered in her own blood, her mind spinning. Pain and shock slowed her instincts, and she had no idea what she should do. The wounds were bleeding badly, and she knew she'd die if she didn't treat them. Her mind told her to run as fast as she could, but if she ran, the bleeding would increase, and she would die. Her head said to make sure he can't attack you again. Her head won, and she stepped forward and ran the blade across his exposed throat, slicing deep through skin, muscle, and vascular matter. Arterial spray splattered onto her face, and he began to writhe and thrash his limbs in the air, his feet pushing him along the corridor, turning in a circle like a dying insect. Kim watched, exhausted and horrified but fascinated by his death throes. She hoped the bastard was suffering. His writhing slowed and eventually stopped. The coppery smell of blood filled the air, mixing with the excrement he was smothered in.

Kim staggered back against the wall and put her hand over the wound beneath her ribs. It was bleeding the most. Her other hand went to her throat. The wound was shallow but bleeding profusely. She staggered back into the room and looked around. There were three rolls of gaffer tape next to the trolley, put there to restrain her no doubt. She picked one up and bit a length off, pressing it over the wound on her neck. It stung, but closed the wound. Her fingers were bleeding, making everything slippery. Kim taped her fingers one at a time to stem the flow. She repeated the process with each stab wound, using several strips the hold the skin together until her bleeding was reduced to a minimum. She let herself slide down the wall, her strength fading fast. He was dead. At least she could die in peace without that pervert touching her. As the darkness engulfed her, she embraced it.

Chapter 41

Ernie took off his clothes and put them into a bin bag. He showered and picked a pair of jeans and a Motorhead T-shirt which buried him, pushing his feet into a pair of Nike trainers. They were too big, but they would do. He found a beanie hat and pulled it down to his eyes. It would cover most of his hair and enough of his face to confuse onlookers. Everyone was a witness these days and everyone carried a camera in their pocket. He made sure there was no one around and left through the front door and walked across the road to the graveyard. The wind picked up, and he wished he'd taken a jacket too. There was a newly dug grave a few hundred yards away at the far side of the cemetery and he walked towards the mound of dark brown soil. The occupant hadn't arrived yet, and he tossed the beanbag into the grave and covered it with soil before jogging across the cemetery towards Maeshyfryd Road. His Jeep was parked on Kings Road, and he kept running until he reached it. The street was quiet and there was nobody around as he unlocked it and climbed in. Ernie started the engine and fastened his seat belt.

He glanced in the rear-view mirror. A police interceptor turned onto the road and stopped in the middle, blocking the road. The ANPR would pick up his plate and if the police were looking for him, it would flag up that he was wanted. There was a chance Helen hadn't spoken to them yet, but it was unlikely. He engaged first gear and pulled out, heading towards the bridge, but as he neared the junction, another police car pulled out from Cleveland Avenue, obstructing him. His car had clearly been spotted earlier, and they were waiting for him to come back to his vehicle. Two more police cars screamed to a halt behind him, and uniformed officers piled out of them, surrounding his Jeep. Ernie thought about ramming the interceptor and squashing the coppers around him, teaching them a lesson not to annoy him when he was working. He had a job to do, protecting his daughter and ensuring his family unit remained intact even if she was encouraging the boy. Slut.

The driver's door was pulled open, and officers began shouting orders at him. One of them told him he was under arrest for assaulting Helen Metcalfe and anything he said would be taken into evidence, blah, blah, blah. He let them put a handcuff on his left wrist and then self-preservation took over.

Ernie head-butted the officer trying to cuff him, breaking his nose. He fell back, impeding the others from reaching into the Jeep. Ernie slammed the door closed and locked it, smiling at the officer desperately trying to open it. He drew his baton ready to smash the glass, but Ernie put the Jeep in gear and drove forwards, aiming at the front of the police car, spinning the front end violently. It created a gap wide enough for him to manoeuvre the Jeep between the interceptor and a row of parked cars, which belonged to the residents. Sirens blared as another vehicle shadowed him. A baton shattered the rear passenger window, but Ernie wasn't stopping for anyone. He swerved around the roadblock and accelerated. He didn't see an officer deploy the stinger which ripped his tyres to bits. The Jeep trundled on, tyres shredding, running on the metal rims, spraying sparks in its wake until one of the front wheels disintegrated and it came to a halt. Ernie opened the door and made a run for it, but a younger faster man caught him and brought him down with a crunching tackle, knocking the wind from his lungs. They cuffed him properly this time and put him into the back of a marked vehicle. Officers spoke to him, asking him questions, but he remained silent. They charged him with assaulting Helen, which was ridiculous. She was his daughter, and it was his job to discipline her. Slut.

CHAPTER 42

Olivia Mann was sitting at Alan's desk reading the updates on her laptop when the desk phone rang. She was preparing her first briefing to the MIT at Holyhead. Chod poked his head around the door and pointed to her phone.

'That's the super from Caernarfon,' he said. 'She has an update for you, apparently. Something to do with the Judge Preece murder.'

'Thanks, Chod,' Olivia said.

'So, it is a murder?' he asked with a cheeky grin on his face.

'As opposed to what?' Olivia asked, frowning.

'A bog-standard hit and run.'

'You know the score,' Olivia said. 'It's a hit and run until we can prove otherwise.'

'Is it connected to our case?' Chod asked. Olivia looked at him and smiled. 'I thought so, too. Too much of a coincidence not to be,' he added. 'I hope you don't mind, but I've been digging around a bit.'

'And what has your digging uncovered?' Olivia asked.

'Nothing yet but I have a few leads on cases where Alan, Kim, and the judge were involved. I'm compiling a list.'

'Good. Thank you for using your initiative.'

'No problem,' Chod said.

'But don't overlook the barrister,' she added. 'Melisa Wilding.'

'Do you think she may have been the target?' Chod asked.

'I don't know who the target was, but until we do, we have to include both of them in our searches.'

'Will do, boss,' Chod said, closing the door behind him.

Olivia picked up the telephone. 'Hello,' she said. 'Superintendent Mann speaking.'

'Olivia, this is Sharon Williams from Caernarfon,' the caller said.

'Hello, Sharon. I didn't realise it would be you working on this,' Olivia said. 'I haven't seen you since the conference in Cardiff.'

'I vaguely remember being there,' Sharon said, laughing. 'I've been asked to keep you up to date by Bill Armstrong.'

'Yes. I asked him to keep me in the loop. The chief wants to keep a lid on this for obvious reasons, but we have to assume your hit and run is connected to the hit on the detectives on Anglesey,' Olivia said.

'We all know it is and a little birdie told me the Daily Post is going to run with it on the front page this morning,' Sharon said.

'The chief won't be happy, but it's about as obvious as it gets,' Olivia said.

'Agreed. We just need to find the link.'

'How's the investigation going?'

'Slowly,' Sharon said. 'A fisherman found a van fitting the description burnt out in the forest near Ruthin this morning, but we think it was taken there directly after the hit and torched. Obviously, they had a getaway vehicle waiting there.'

'Ruthin is on the way to the main routes out of North Wales,' Olivia said. 'Chester, Liverpool, and Manchester are all less than an hour from there.'

'That's what we're working on,' Sharon said. 'We're looking at anyone who was sent down by Preece, linked to Alan Williams or Kim Davies, who's been released in the last month. Unfortunately, she sent a lot of people away and their arrest and conviction figures were top drawer, so we're ploughing through the data.'

'And what about Wilding?' Olivia asked. 'She could have been the target.'

'We're looking into both. Don't worry,' Sharon said. 'If there's a link, we'll find it, eventually.'

'I think there's a trigger,' Olivia said.

'Trigger?'

'Yes. Something has happened recently which has triggered this series of attacks,' Olivia said.

'Such as?'

'Have you heard of the Eccles brothers?' Olivia asked.

'They run an outfit in Manchester?' Sharon said. 'A big one.'

'That's them,' Olivia said. 'I was working on the case until they were found murdered on Saddleworth Moor. They'd been tortured before they were murdered and men like that know a lot of valuable information. They could have disclosed something which has had a knock-on effect.'

'Like ripples in a pond,' Sharon said.

'Exactly. Kim Davies was taken either because of something she's done or something she knows, and it may have been exposed when the Eccles brothers were interrogated.'

'I have to agree,' Sharon said. 'But identifying it is proving to be time-consuming because we don't know what we're looking for.'

'They could have killed her and left her body in her house, but they took her, which tells me they needed her alive. So, someone thinks she knows something and wants to interrogate her, or Kim has done something and they want to punish her face to face, which makes it personal,' Olivia said. 'Something triggered this, and I need to know what it is.' A knock on her door interrupted her. 'Can I call you back? It's like a madhouse here.'

'No problem,' Sharon said. 'I might have specifics and not just theories by then. Speak later.'

'Okay, thanks for the call. Come in,' Olivia said, ending the call. Bob Dewhurst, Richard, and Chod stepped in, looking worried. 'You three look like you're bearing bad news?'

'We've got another case which is going to need our attention. We'll let Bob explain,' Richard said.

'Hello, Bob,' Olivia said. 'I'm Superintendent Mann, but you can call me Olivia.'

'Nice to meet you, Olivia,' Bob said. 'Welcome to Anglesey. It smells better in here,' he added.

'Thank you.'

'Is that Jo Malone, Mimosa and Cardamom?' Bob asked. Chod and Richard laughed.

'It is,' Olivia said, smiling.

'Eileen wears it,' Bob said. 'She's the better half.'

'I gathered,' Olivia said. 'She has good taste in perfume. Now then, what are you looking so worried about?'

'We've got another body and another man seriously injured,' Bob said.

'Connected to our investigation?'

'No. Not that I can see, but you need to know all the same. The victim is Ben Willis, known locally as Wills. He's been tortured and beaten to death in his living room.'

'Here in Holyhead?'

'Yes. Treseifion Estate.'

'And you say he was tortured?' Olivia asked.

'Yes. His fingers were crushed with a hammer, so I'm assuming someone was asking him questions he didn't want to answer,' Bob said. 'Then they used the hammer to cave his skull in.'

'Who found him?'

'His ex-wife,' Bob said. 'And his eight-year-old son.'

'Oh no,' Olivia said. 'Poor kid.'

'To compound matters, his best friend, Paul Conor, was found in his back garden with his head cracked open by a garden spade. He lives a few streets away near the graveyard.'

'Is he alive?' Olivia asked.

'Barely,' Bob said.

'And you think they're linked?'

'The thing is, they're both close friends with a man called Jimmy Woods.' Olivia looked confused. 'Let me explain. Woods's son was attacked outside his school at Menai Bridge yesterday. We investigated it because we knew all the Dicks were tied up. The boy identified a man called Ernest Metcalfe as his attacker before retracting his statement later in the day.'

'I'm following,' Olivia said.

'Metcalfe has just been arrested for assaulting his thirteen-year-old daughter,' Bob explained. 'Apparently, he deleted all her social media accounts before he broke her cheekbone. He left the house in a rage and his mother took the girl to casualty and they called social services and they called us.'

'And you think the murder and the assault are connected to this Metcalfe chap?' Olivia said, nodding.

'Wills, Conor, and Woods are thick as thieves,' Bob said. 'It can't be a coincidence that Woods's boy is allegedly assaulted by Metcalfe, then Woods's friends are attacked.' Bob shrugged. 'You can see where I'm going with this.'

'Absolutely, I can,' Olivia said. 'Both men were attacked in their homes?'

'Yes,' Bob said.

'That takes a special kind of dangerous man to go to someone's home and attack them,' Olivia said. 'And torture is a specialist thing. Definitely not for the squeamish.' She steepled her fingers beneath her chin. 'Can there be another explanation? Is there any connection between these men and OCG activity?'

'Not a chance,' Chod said. 'These guys are rarely sober enough to get themselves home at night, let alone run an operation.'

'Do we have any witnesses to tie Metcalfe to these attacks?' Olivia asked.

'Not yet. We've got officers going door to door.'

'Was there any trace at the scenes?'

'Not yet,' Bob said. 'Metcalfe is ex-forces and ex-military police. He's forensically savvy.'

'Chod, take your team and investigate this,' Olivia said. 'This Metcalfe character can't be allowed back on the streets until we're sure he didn't do it.'

CHAPTER 43

Jimmy Woods looked white as a sheet when he ended the call. Rio and Wendy were sitting on the settee, waiting for him to explain what had happened. Lisa Willis had called him twenty-minutes ago and the one-sided conversation sounded very grim. Something bad had happened, and it was linked to what had happened to Rio. They could gauge that much. Jimmy looked at them and wiped a tear from the corner of his eye.

'What's happened?' Wendy asked. She reached out and touched Rio, instinctively protecting her child. Rio moved closer to his mother.

'Wills is dead,' Jimmy said. 'Lisa found him in the living room. Little Jon was there too.'

'Oh, my Lord,' Wendy said. 'What happened to him?'

'She's not sure yet, but he's been murdered,' Jimmy said. 'The police won't tell her anything, as she's not his next of kin anymore.'

'How bloody stupid can they be? She's the mother of his kid. What exactly did she say, Jimmy?'

'He was attacked with a hammer,' Jimmy said, sparing them the details. 'He was a mess. Someone really did him over.'

'Everyone likes Wills,' Wendy said. 'Who would do something like that to him?'

'I've got a fucking good idea who it was,' Jimmy muttered. He thought about what to say and how to say it. 'I think Metcalfe did him in.'

'Fucking hell,' Wendy said. The implications hit her. She held Rio's hand. 'That's a confident shout. What makes you say that?'

'Listen to me, Rio,' Jimmy said, sitting down opposite him. 'Wills was murdered and Conor was attacked with a spade in his back garden early this morning. They are not coincidences. Not for one minute do I think it's not connected to Metcalfe.'

'For the love of God,' Wendy muttered. She went to the cupboard and took out her emergency packet of cigarettes. The lighter was stuffed inside. They looked old and stale. She'd been off them for three years. 'What the fuck is wrong with that man?'

'Mum, you've packed in,' Rio said. 'Don't smoke.'

'Shut up, Rio. This is all because you're trying to fuck his daughter and she's thirteen.' Rio looked horrified his mouth open. 'Don't look at me like that. Don't think I don't know what you watch on your computer.'

'Wendy!' Jimmy said. 'There's no need for that. The poor lad is cringing there.'

'It's true. Watching porn night and day, wanking himself stupid.'

'Mum!' Rio snapped, blushing bright purple.

'Who do you think washes your sheets?' she argued. 'The spunk-stain fairy?'

'Oh my God,' Rio said, putting his head in his hands. 'Are you actually my mum?'

'He's thinking with his knob and look where it's got us,' Wendy said, shaking her head. 'He takes after you.'

'Oh, here we go!' Jimmy shouted. 'Every time he fucks up, he takes after me.'

'Well, you're the biggest fuck up on the planet and you're his dad, so it makes perfect sense to me,' Wendy said.

'Will you stop arguing just for once?' Rio moaned. He put his head in his hands again. 'I can't cope with you two.'

'I'm struggling to cope myself as it happens. Tell us what you think's going on in plain English.' Wendy lit up, ignoring her son's complaints.

'Wills was battered to death with a hammer and Conor was smashed in the face with a spade,' Jimmy said, shrugging. 'I know they're not everyone's favourite people, but they didn't deserve that.' He paused. 'No one in this town has a grudge against them to the extent they would kill them, which means there's another reason for this.' Jimmy pointed at Rio. 'It can only be because of what happened to Rio. This is Metcalfe. I'd put my house on it.'

'You don't have a house,' Wendy said. 'You lost that when you decided Guinness was more important than us.'

'Funny fucker,' Jimmy said, frowning.

'The truth hurts, hey, Jimmy?'

'Two of my best mates have been attacked. One of them is dead, the other is fighting for his life so can we leave the sarcastic comments for another time?'

'With a bit of luck, you'll be next.' Jimmy rolled his eyes and sighed.

'Sorry,' Wendy muttered, drawing deep on her cigarette. It was stale and tasted like shit. She stubbed it out on the packet. 'I'm stressing here. Why do you think this was Metcalfe?'

'Who else could it be?' Jimmy said.

'I don't know, but I can't see why he would just attack them because they're your mates,' Wendy said. 'What had made him attack them?'

'I'm not sure…'

'I can tell by your face you're lying to us,' Wendy said. 'What are you not telling us?'

'Nothing.'

'Get out if you're going to keep on lying.'

'Wills was following him.'

'What?'

'You know what he's like. He thinks he's Sherlock Holmes when something is going on.'

'Why was he following him?'

'Conor wanted to batter him for what he did to Rio,' Jimmy said. 'He said we had to do him in, and Wills was following him to see if there was a pattern to his movements.'

'"A pattern to his movements"?' Wendy said, shaking her head. 'I've heard it all now. So, Wills was following the man and you think he's twigged that he was being followed?' Wendy asked.

'Pretty much,' Jimmy said, nodding.

'I'm not surprised,' Wendy said. 'Wills has gone beyond his skill sets there.'

'He's dead, Wendy,' Jimmy said. 'You shouldn't speak ill of the dead.'

'Why not?' she asked. 'Your dad was a complete wanker, and I told him when he was alive, so what's the problem now?'

'For fuck's sake.' Jimmy sighed. 'Do you ever take five minutes off from being a knobhead?'

'Not when you're around,' Wendy said. 'I can't help myself.'

'Are you sure Wills was following him, Dad?' Rio asked, tiring of his mother's sarcasm.

'Yes. He told us he was going to follow him on his bike,' Jimmy said. 'He must have got too close, and Metcalfe spotted him. I can't think of any other valid reason why anyone would hurt Wills.' He thought for a moment. 'Conor is a different matter. Half the town would queue up to smack him in the face with a shovel, but not Wills.'

'So, we're going to take it from what you've said, that Metcalfe realised Wills was following him and found out where he lived and asked him why he was following him?' Wendy asked.

'Yes.' Jimmy nodded.

'Do the police know this?'

'No.'

'Idiot. Well, you need to tell them.'

'We need to calm down and think about this,' Jimmy said. 'Because this guy is a fucking psycho. The only thing that connects them to Metcalfe is Rio. We need to think about Rio,' Jimmy added. 'He went to the hospital to grab him and threaten him. This bloke doesn't give a fuck.'

'He retracted his statement,' Wendy said.

'Yes. I did,' Rio said, scared. 'I'm not saying anything to the police. He'll come and get you and Mum.'

'They'll come here when they put two and two together and as a family, we're saying fuck all,' Jimmy said. 'This man is twisted, and we don't want him pissed off with us. We walk away from this now and we stay schtum, understand?'

Chapter 44

Braden Murphy was shivering so hard he thought his teeth were going to crack as they chattered against each other. He was naked and fastened to a chair with zip ties. His feet were in a tin bath, which had been filled with water, and he could no longer feel his legs. The numbness had spread to his hips, making them ache so much it felt like they were on fire. His fingers tingled as if ice moved through his veins. Next to him on the left was a trolley which held a selection of medical scalpels, bone saws, stainless steel pliers, dental drills, and a blowtorch. To his right was a dolly which carried a huge lorry battery and some jump leads. He'd been sitting there for hours and hours with no communication from his captors, despite his protestations. Thirst meant he could no longer shout.

He had been a judge in Dublin long enough to know he'd been kidnapped by a paramilitary organisation. For what purpose, he didn't know. This was standard procedure. Tie up the victim and leave them cold and hungry with the tools of torture in plain sight. Exhaustion and the sheer terror of the anticipation of those tools being used was enough to break any man even before the first question was asked. Braden had sent many members from all sides to prison, showing no prejudice for protestant or catholic. He'd tried to be a fair judge and had never taken a bribe, although there had been more offers than he could remember. The sound of a door slamming and footsteps approaching reached him. His heart began pounding in his chest and terror made it difficult to breathe.

A woman he vaguely recognised and four men wearing balaclavas came into view. He couldn't place the woman, but he knew he'd seen her before.

'Who are you?' Braden asked. 'Why am I here?'

'Because you're Braden Murphy,' the woman said. 'Judge Braden Murphy.' She lit a cigarette. 'Do you remember me?'

'I can't say I do,' Braden said, shivering. 'Should I?'

'Probably not,' she said. 'My name is Veronica Kelly. My son was Niall Kelly.'

'I remember him,' Braden said, nodding. 'He had a cache of arms in a lock-up and was plotting to raid a depository near Kilkenny.'

'He didn't have a lock-up, and he didn't have any weapons,' Veronica said. 'He was twenty-one and didn't even own the car he drove. But I'm glad you remember him.'

'Is that what this is all about?' Braden asked. She nodded and inhaled on the cigarette. 'I had no influence on the jury in that case,' he said. 'The evidence was overwhelming. My hands are tied, excuse the pun, when it comes to sentencing. He had automatic weapons and hand grenades. The sentences are mandatory.'

'He didn't have any weapons, or a lock-up,' Veronica said. 'That's the point.'

'You say that as his mother, but I have to make my decision based on the evidence presented in court and the evidence was irrefutable,' Braden said. 'The surveillance from the mainland was damning if I remember rightly?'

'It was manufactured to show what they wanted it to show.'

'There were several warrants signed by a judge in Caernarfon, presented by North Wales Police. The chain of evidence was uncompromised,' Braden said. 'It certainly showed your son in a poor light.'

'There were powerful men behind that operation, not a twenty-one-year-old. He was the fall guy,' Veronica said. 'And you know it.'

'I can't read between the lines. There are no grey areas and his association with the paramilitaries was clear,' Braden said. 'He's one of thousands who've been led astray by these people.' He gestured to the men in balaclavas. 'Yourself included. The apple didn't fall far from the tree, did it?'

'He was found hanging last week,' Veronica said. The words were like a punch in the guts. He knew then he was in deep trouble. Braden shook his head and closed his eyes. 'They're saying it was suicide, but we all know how it works inside. He had too much information to trade, so they silenced him just in case he decided to make a deal to shorten his sentence.' She stubbed out the cigarette with her shoe. 'You could have stipulated he served his time in segregation. He was just a boy in his head.'

'He was a twenty-one-year-old man in the eyes of the law,' Braden said. 'I had no choice but to treat him as such.'

'He wasn't tough enough to survive in a prison surrounded by wolves. They ate him alive from day one. You as good as hanged him yourself.'

'Hindsight is a wonderful thing,' Braden said, sighing. 'I'm so sorry for your loss. Truly I am, but I'm just human and we sometimes make the wrong call. Had I thought he was in peril, I would have protected him, but he was part of an organisation who look after themselves, especially inside. Most of them don't serve hard time, it's like a holiday camp for them.'

'A holiday camp where the guests are hanged with electrical flex, which was pulled so tight it nearly decapitated him?' She shrugged. 'I went to the post-mortem. It's not something a mother should see, but I had to because you accepted that he could be in charge of a multimillion Euro heist, owned automatic weapons, and would have an easy time inside?'

'I can't change it now as much as I would love to. What do you want from me?' Braden asked. His top lip began to quiver. 'How can I fix this?'

'Fix it?' she said, shaking her head. 'You can't fix it, but I can watch you suffering for a while when they fry your testicles with those jump leads before they dismember you like an old doll. It won't fix anything, but it will make me feel better for a while.'

A Disturbing Thing Happened Today

Chapter 45

Vince used the grab to lift the burnt-out van onto the flatbed truck. The roof squealed and the sound of metal on metal filled the woods. It was a painstaking operation, but finally, it was done. The CSIs were covering it up, and they were being very precious about it, too. It would take them an hour to do a five-minute job. They always did. Don't touch this and don't touch that. Be careful with this and be careful with that; it was as if he was five years old. Until he discovered the secrets of making things levitate, he had to fucking touch things and he had to fucking move things. He couldn't reinvent the laws of physics just to please them. Silly fuckers. It would take them at least another half an hour to put their covers over the vehicle. They had to use their own, of course, to stop cross contamination. He wouldn't mind all the fuss, but the van was a scorched metal shell. It was impossible to distinguish what make it was, never mind recover evidence. The seats had been reduced to metal springs, the dashboard was a blackened puddle in the footwell, and all the paintwork inside and out was gone. It was a galvanised metal frame full of ash. Having watched a lot of *CSI Miami*, he knew they were recovering fuck all from the wreck, so why be so precious about it?

A Disturbing Thing Happened Today

Vince needed a shit, and he couldn't wait any longer. He walked away from the truck and ducked beneath some low branches. The forest floor sloped away down to the water's edge. Llyn Brenig was a huge lake, actually a man-made reservoir built to protect the water supply to Liverpool. It was usually busy with trout fishermen, paddle boarders, sailors, and walkers, but the weather was shockingly bad. The wind and rain had put off all but the hardiest adventurer. He neared the water and identified a secluded spot to squat. A rotten smell drifted to him. He wrinkled his nose and looked around for the cause of the stench. Floating at the water's edge was the bloated body of a man. The skin was slimy and grey, the beard entangled with pondweed. Vince forgot all about his crap and ran back up the slope to tell the police.

Chapter 46

The MIT was gathered for a briefing in the operations room at Holyhead. Most of the sixty detectives on the case were present. Olivia Mann had introduced herself as the new senior investigation officer and summarised where they were up to. She walked to the screen wall and pointed to the biggest image. Her hair was tied up in a ponytail, her make-up to the minimum, and she presented as a professional individual with striking aesthetics.

'This footage is from a doorbell video on the Gorad Road and this one is from another camera across the A5, on Station Road here,' she said, pointing to a second screen. 'They show two identical white vans passing within minutes of each other. Four hours later, they're seen going in the opposite direction at speed. We're working on getting the plates enhanced, but there must be more footage of these vans in the area. I want as many officers as we can spare finding camera footage. Uniform canvassed the Gorad Estate, and no one has any work being carried out, no construction, no cleaning, no gardening,' she said. 'So, what are these vans doing there?'

'Traffic sometimes cuts through Gorad to the Cemaes Road,' a detective said. 'But it's unlikely.'

'So, until we know differently, these vehicles are our focus.' She looked at the faces in the room. They were glued to the screens and listening intently to what she was saying. She had their attention, one-hundred per cent. 'We need to know if they left the island or if they're still here,' Olivia said. 'The van used in the hit and run in Caernarfon was a hire van from Liverpool, taken from this depot on Bath Street, off the Dock Road. It was found burnt out in the forest near Llyn Brenig, which says to me they were heading back to Liverpool. Maybe theses vans were from the same area. Let's check if any vehicles matching these were hired out that day, please.'

'We can take all the footage from the bridges,' Richard said. 'If they left the island, we'll know.'

'Okay. How long will that take?'

'A few days,' Richard said.

'Let's get a bigger team on it and make it a day?' Olivia said. 'How many people do you need?'

'Four to do it in a day.'

'Get on it,' Olivia said. 'The other way off the island is through the port. I want a team checking CCTV and manifests for that day and the day after. Ferries, cargo ships, trawlers, everything that floats.'

'It would be difficult to take a hostage on the ferries, even tied up in the boot. The checks are random, but it would be a gamble.'

'Surely, they've customised their vehicles to suit their purpose. Come on, use your imagination,' Olivia said. 'We all know how much contraband goes through this port and it isn't on the back seat of a car. These criminals are determined and inventive. We need to think like them.'

'I think you're right to focus on Ireland. We've just got the results of the financials for Brandon Tanner,' Annie said, staring at her laptop. 'Tanner had the sum of ten grand paid into his business account from the Bank of Ireland in Kilkenny.'

'Any details?'

'Providing a service,' Annie said.

'Ah,' Olivia said. 'That changes the perspective of things.' She turned to Richard. 'Hold off on the bridge footage. Put one person on it and change focus to the port. We have a weapon which was probably last in service in Ireland and now the man found with the weapon in his hand has ten grand in his account from the Bank of Ireland. I don't think they crossed the bridge.'

'No problem, I agree,' Richard said.

'Chod, call the super in Caernarfon,' Olivia said. 'Tell her there's a high probability of an Irish connection. It might narrow down their search and cross reference your lists with her, please.'

'On it like a car bonnet,' Chod said, smiling. He picked up his desk phone and dialled. Olivia hid a smile. His enthusiasm was admirable, if not amusing. 'Leave it to me,' he added as he dialled.

'Do we have anything from the CSIs yet?'

'Nothing yet, but I'll call Pamela Stone now,' Richard said.

'I have a feeling Brandon Tanner didn't pull that trigger,' Olivia said. 'Let's knuckle down on this and meet back at six o'clock.'

The meeting broke up and Olivia made a point of working the room, talking to each team of detectives as she went. The atmosphere was tense, but positive. It took her nearly an hour to talk to each group individually.

'Boss,' Chod called, waving a hand. 'You're not going to believe this.'

'I probably will,' she said.

'The recovery team at Llyn Brenig has found a body in the reservoir near where the van was burnt out,' he said. 'There's no ID, but he has a four-leaf clover tattoo with Irish Pride written around it.'

'Cause of death?'

'A bullet to the back of the head.'

CHAPTER 47

Ernest Metcalfe was sitting in the interview room, flanked by his solicitor, who was young but had experience of criminal cases. The nearest stables of serious crime briefs were in Chester. Ernie was calm on the exterior. His appearance was one of a man with no issues about his behaviour, no fear of prosecution, and no concerns about being remanded in custody. Inside was turmoil, anger, and aggression. Chod walked into the room accompanied by Zoe Baxter, a detective sergeant from St Asaph. They sat down and Chod went through the legalities of the interview and cued the cameras.

'Are you okay if we call you Ernie?' Chod asked.

'That's my name.' Ernie looked disinterested. 'Call me what you like, but let's make this quick.'

'Do you want to start by telling us what happened with your daughter, Helen?' Chod began.

'She's been acting very naively lately, and she's only thirteen, still a child,' Ernie said. 'Older boys are circling and sending inappropriate messages, mostly on social media, and so I deleted her profiles to protect her.' He shrugged.

'Did you see these messages, or did she tell you about them?' Zoe asked.

'I saw them.'

'On her device or on your own?' Zoe pressed. 'Have you hacked her accounts?'

'I haven't hacked anything,' Ernie said, shaking his head. 'I bought software so I can monitor her communications.'

'So, you've bugged her phone?' Chod asked. 'I bet she was mad about that?'

'She's thirteen and boys are trying to fuck her. What am I supposed to do?' Ernie said, angrily.

'You're supposed to protect her,' Chod said, nodding. 'I can see that.' Chod sat back. 'Was Helen encouraging them?'

'I beg your pardon?' Ernie said, swallowing his anger.

'You know what I mean,' Chod said. 'Was there a bit of flirting going on?'

'Absolutely not,' Ernie lied. 'I told her that I'd deleted her accounts for her own good. She took it badly and became hysterical and abusive, which I'm not used to.'

'Do you have a good relationship with her?' Zoe asked.

'Yes, of course. I bring them up on my own since my wife died and it's a struggle sometimes.'

'I can imagine,' Chod said. 'I have three boys. Pain in the arse sometimes, but we wouldn't change that, would we?'

'No.'

'So, you bugged her phone and saw a bit of flirting going on and lost your marbles?' Chod summarised.

'That is not what I said.' Ernie was fighting to keep control. He wanted to punch the detective in the face. 'I said she was behaving irrationally and swearing at me. She called me a dick, and I slapped her face.' Ernie looked apologetic. 'It wasn't meant to be hard. She fell off the chair and banged her face on her desk. I didn't mean to knock her off the chair. She was unbalanced and fell.'

'She has a broken cheekbone,' Zoe interrupted. 'Which takes a considerable amount of force.'

'What can I say?' Ernie said, shrugging. 'I slapped her, and she fell against the desk. Charge me, so I can go home to my children.'

'Your children are subject to a child protection order at the moment,' Zoe said. 'They're with your mother for now, but you can't see them until social services are happy that you're not a danger to them.'

'I'm their father,' Ernie said, flushing red. 'I'm not a danger to them. I protect them.'

'And one of your daughters is in hospital,' Zoe said. 'You put her there.'

'I think we've established that,' his brief said. 'Are you going to charge Mr Metcalfe?'

'All in good time,' Chod said. He smiled at Ernie. 'You were spoken to briefly yesterday by a couple of uniformed officers about the assault on Rio Woods at Menai Bridge.'

'Yes. They were mistaken.'

'You said you were at home in bed when the assault happened,' Chod said. 'Your mother gave you an alibi.'

'Is there a question there?' the brief asked.

'Your daughter said she didn't actually see you when they left for school,' Chod said. 'You spoke to them through the door.'

'I'm sorry,' the brief said. 'Question?'

'Was Rio Woods the older boy "circling Helen", as you put it?' Chod asked. 'Is he trying to fuck her?'

'Can we rein it in a bit?' the brief complained.

'I'm using your client's words,' Chod said. 'I would be furious if it was my daughter.' He looked at Ernie. Ernie stared back. 'Is that what happened? You saw a message from Rio Woods and lost your shit?'

'I don't know the boy,' Ernie said.

'He knows you and he knows Helen.'

'Hasn't he withdrawn his allegation?'

'How would you know that?' Chod asked.

'Know what?'

'How would you know that he's withdrawn his allegation?' Chod asked. 'We haven't told you that yet.'

'Because you haven't charged me,' Ernie said, blushing again. 'Are you going to charge me with his assault?'

'You assaulted him because he was messaging your daughter,' Chod said. 'So, you went to his school and beat him up.'

'That's rubbish,' Ernie said. 'You haven't got a shred of evidence, not even a statement from the victim.' Chod looked him in the eye, but he didn't flinch. 'I'm sure you've checked the GPS on my phone. It will prove I was in Trearddur Bay and I have four witnesses who will put me at home in my bed.'

'Behind a closed door,' Chod added.

'I'm not a fucking magician and I can't throw my voice,' Ernie said. 'Do I have to listen to this shit?' he asked his brief.

'I think you need to stop fishing and charge my client with whatever you have.'

'Where did you go when you left home last night?' Chod asked. Ernie didn't show any emotion. 'After you sparked out your daughter.'

'Detective Hall!' the brief warned. 'That's antagonistic at best.'

'Where did you go?' Zoe pressed. Ernie looked at her, head tilted to the side like a confused dog.

'We found Ben Willis beaten to death in his home this morning,' Chod said.

'Ben who?'

'Willis,' Zoe said. 'Actually, his ex-wife and eight-year-old son found him with his brains bashed out.'

'I've never heard of him,' Ernie said.

'He's very good friends with Rio's father,' Zoe said. 'The boy you didn't assault.'

'That's enough,' the brief said. 'Charge Mr Metcalfe, or we walk right now.'

'Why did you park your Jeep on Kings Road?' Chod asked. 'That's where we arrested you.'

'I went for a walk,' Ernie said. 'I like walking down Plas Road towards the coast.'

'You live across the road from the sea in Trearddur Bay and yet you drove to Kings Road to walk along Plas Road?' Chod said, frowning. 'Sounds like a load of bollocks to me.'

'On that note, we're ending this interview immediately.'

'Okay,' Chod said. 'We're going to charge you with a section eighteen assault on Helen Metcalfe and we'll be holding you in custody at Caernarfon pending further enquiries regarding the murder of Ben Willis and a serious assault on another male.' Ernie folded his arms and sat back in his chair. 'Do you have anything to say?'

'My client won't be making any further comments,' the brief said. 'And I will be opposing the request to extend custody on the grounds of you having nothing to connect my client to the murder of Ben Willis.'

'You know you did it,' Chod said. 'And I know you did it. Your brief is clutching at straws. Tell us what happened.'

'No comment,' Ernie said, smiling. He flicked his middle finger in Chod's face. 'Is this yours?'

Chapter 48

Alan was drifting in and out of reality, pain his constant companion. He floated upwards towards consciousness and then the morphine driver would kick in and send him spinning back down into the warm darkness. It wasn't a frightening place. It was far nicer than consciousness. His sister had been to see him, although he knew she had died years before when lung cancer decimated her. She smoked all through her illness up to the point where she could no longer be pushed outside in a wheelchair to have one. When she coughed, it sounded like her lungs were full of phlegm, almost as if they were flooded. She died before his mother did, but she was too ill to be told at the time. There was little point in her suffering the grief when she was at death's door herself. When she came to him, she was radiant and young and pretty. Her presence brought an overwhelming aura of wellbeing. He felt happy to see her looking so well, despite knowing she couldn't really be there. She was.

The atmosphere changed when he heard Kim calling for help. She was in a dark corner somewhere, but he couldn't see her. He turned around in a circle until he felt dizzy, but she was nowhere to be seen. Her voice echoed, tainted with fear. He tried to call to her, but his voice wouldn't work how he wanted it to. Why was she here in this nether world he wandered through? There was only one answer, but he didn't like it. She'd been missing. He remembered that much. Her voice called out again, and he felt her fear. Wherever she was, she was terrified.

Chapter 49

ACC Bill Armstrong and Chief Constable Diane Warburton were in the headquarters at St Asaph, listening to Olivia via a Teams connection. Pamela Stone and Rob Wilkinson were at their lab on the Wirral and were also in the meeting.

'There was no gunshot residue on Tanner's hands,' Rob said. 'It's an old gun and a revolver, which means the ammunition ports are open, so at the point of firing, GSR is expelled all over the hand. We'd expect to see a lot of residue on whoever pulled the trigger, and Tanner had none. He didn't kill himself, someone else pulled the trigger.'

'That model of weapon last saw service in Ireland,' Olivia added. 'It was a British Army service revolver phased out in the thirties and there were hundreds left behind. The paramilitaries have been using these ever since, and they've popped up all over the place through the decades of violence. They're old but they do the job at close range, so I think they brought it with them knowing they were going to leave it behind.' Olivia shrugged. 'Why leave a new Glock when you have an obsolete one to hand?'

'There's certainly a lot of evidence backing up your theory. A large sum of money was paid into his bank from Ireland?' Bill asked.

'Yes, into a business account,' Olivia said. 'From the Bank of Ireland in Kilkenny.'

'How much?' Diane asked.

'Ten thousand pounds.'

'There were four contraptions, including the one they deployed?' Diane asked.

'Yes. Two and half grand each sounds like a reasonable price,' Bill said. 'Have we tied the Caernarfon incident into the mix yet?'

'The van used was burnt out and dumped. The driver executed with a bullet to the back of the head. The van was hired in Liverpool near the Dock Road,' Pamela said. 'And the other two vans have been identified as hire vehicles taken from the city too. The body recovered from Llyn Brenig has been identified as Liam O'Grady from Dublin,' she continued. 'He has a single bullet wound to the back of the head, execution style.'

'The hire depots are walking distance from the Dublin Ferry Port,' Olivia added. 'We identified the plates from video footage and the same vehicles were aboard the Sealink Ferry from Holyhead which sailed at three the morning after Kim was taken,' Olivia explained. 'We've sent the details to the Garda in Dublin, but they're not very responsive and even less hopeful of us finding them.'

'What did they say?' Diane asked, raising an eyebrow.

'They said they would be stripped and sold for parts and the identifiable bits melted down for scrap and that no one in their right minds would be still driving them around Dublin. You can see where we're going with this,' Olivia said. 'O'Grady bought a ticket as a foot passenger and then took a taxi to the hire depot. He was with another man, who we haven't identified yet but the Garda said O'Grady was on the periphery of the Real IRA but was also an informer on their payroll, so it looks like they sent him on a mission to kill Judge Preece and Melisa Wilding and then shot him in the head. Three birds with one stone, if you like.' She shrugged. 'It's clear someone high up in the chain of command has authorised these hits.'

'Hits on the mainland like this are almost unheard of. It's political suicide,' Bill agreed.

'Exactly, so I think this is not about politics or policing.' She paused. 'There's a trigger to this, and it's personal,' Olivia added.

'And what do you think the trigger is?' Diane asked.

'That's what we don't know yet,' Olivia said.

'We're not going to get a lot of joy from our Irish friends with what we have,' Diane said.

'It couldn't be clearer where the aggressors have come from and gone to,' Olivia protested. 'Detective Inspector Kim Davies was kidnapped and taken by ferry to Dublin. If she's still alive, she's in Ireland.'

'And which side took here?' Diane asked.

'We don't know.'

'We need to know. By whom and why was she taken?' Diane asked. 'They're the first questions they'll ask.' She shook her head. 'What do you suggest I say?'

'There must be some chatter going on,' Olivia said. 'There's always chatter. Surely their CID or Special Branch should be aware of what's going on?'

'They are aware, Olivia. As soon as I knew, they knew,' Diane said. 'This isn't amateur hour.'

'I'm not saying that.'

'They've been fighting the paramilitaries for decades and the buggers have become very good at not creating chatter unless they want to be heard,' Diane said. 'They're playing a waiting game on this one.'

'Waiting for what, a body?'

'Maybe,' Diane said. 'You've done a good job, Olivia, but we're missing some vital pieces of the puzzle and Kim Davies has been taken beyond our reach. Find me what I need to make this their investigation and demand the Garda act on our behalf. I need more.'

CHAPTER 50

Veronica sipped on her whiskey and flicked through a photograph album, looking at images of Niall from when he was a baby onward. His father had vanished when he was just two. She had a good idea what happened to him and why. He'd run a successful haulage company and made a lot of money, which he invested in property. The paramilitaries on both sides pressured him to help them shift contraband and weapons from the south to the north and to the mainland, but he wouldn't listen to their propositions. Even when they ramped up the pressure and became threatening, he didn't budge. One day he didn't come home, and his car was found abandoned near the border. He was never seen again. Although he left her a wealthy woman, his death left her vulnerable with a small child to bring up, so she did the only thing she could do and accepted the protection of the catholic forces in return for smuggling their shipments. She had spent her lifetime embedded in their operations and became a senior advisor. When he became an adult, Niall had naturally wanted to become a member, despite her resistance to it. The way he saw it, his father had been murdered for his stance and his mother was an integral part of the organisation. It was the natural thing to do.

Her phone rang. Not her personal one, a burner. She rolled her eyes, wanting to be alone with her thoughts, but when the burner rang, it had to be answered.

'What?' she asked.

'They're onto where the detective was taken,' the man said.

'That was quick,' she said. 'You must have left clues.'

'Clues.' He chuckled. 'This isn't a game of Cluedo, Veronica. I told you it was too rushed. Hiring vans and bringing them back to the island by ferry wasn't leaving clues, it was telegraphing where she was taken in big fuck-off-letters.' He paused. 'Killing judges will get you noticed, and you've killed two, so don't be disappointed if the Brits come knocking on the door asking who the fuck killed their detectives.'

'They have nothing,' Veronica said.

'I wouldn't be so sure. I had a call from our friend in Dublin. The Welsh police know the vans went on the ferry and they want them found and the money transfer from Kilkenny has underlined their suspicions.'

'It was sent from Kilkenny because we don't operate there, genius,' Veronica said. 'They have a lot of supposition pointing to Ireland but nothing of substance pointing directly at us,' she said, sipping her drink. 'It's not like you to panic. What's the problem?'

'Des Curran is the problem,' the man said. 'He's a fucking liability. The man is a pervert, and I don't trust him.'

'I know. You made your point, but we were shorthanded,' Veronica said. 'Just don't use him again.'

'He's not answering his phone, and he hasn't been to pick up his money,' the man said. 'He's normally the first in the queue.'

'He's probably on a bender, spending his bonus,' she said. 'He'll get in touch when he's skint.'

'I don't like it,' the man said. 'He had a hard on for that detective and he knows we left her there fastened up.' Veronica remained silent. 'I wouldn't put it past him to go back and give her one.'

'Seriously?' Veronica asked.

'He has a track record of hurting women. That's the type of scumbag he is. He would get off on that type of thing.'

'Fucking hell,' Veronica said. 'If he fucks this up, I'll have him skinned alive.'

'She's fastened to a trolley and locked up, but she's still going to be strong enough to be a handful if he unlocks her. If she gets out of there, we're fucked.'

'You're overthinking this,' Veronica said.

'She knows who you are and why she was brought here.'

'What do you think we should do?' Veronica asked.

'I'll go back and make sure everything is secure,' the man said. 'I think we should move her anyway, just to be on the safe side.'

'Move her where?'

'Probably best if you don't know.' The man chuckled. 'Leave it with me. If Des is there, I'll sort them both out.'

Chapter 51

Helen Metcalfe took a selfie of her swollen face and looked at it. She was beside herself at how she looked. Her eye was closed and almost purple. Her father was a nutjob, and that was a fact. He had attacked Rio, although he denied it. How did he know Rio was messaging her? That was driving her insane. Her phone beeped. It was Rhian. Her text messaging was working, and she'd messaged some of her friends, who were horrified by what had happened and they told her that social media was buzzing about what her dad had done. It was causing a lot of speculation and debate. Helen was gutted she couldn't see it. She felt like her right arm was missing without Facebook. It was like being in a black hole while the best gossip ever was being shared.

Another friend messaged her and said Rio Woods had joined the conversation online. He had posted pictures of his broken nose and was asking if she was okay. Helen said to tell him she was sorry that her father had attacked him, then her friend said he was asking if he could have her number. He wanted her to text him. Helen said she wouldn't text him, but he could text her. She felt excited when she said yes. She held her phone tightly and within seconds, it buzzed.

The message was from an unrecognised number. It was Rio. She stared at the unopened message, her heart thumping in her chest. She couldn't ignore it. She didn't want to ignore it and her father was in the cells, so what could he do? She opened it and read his message, a smile spreading across her face. How could feeling like this be wrong?

Chapter 52

Patrick Finley arrived at the bunker two hours after speaking to Veronica. He took the back roads most of the way, avoiding police patrols and CCTV. Des Curran still wasn't answering his phone, which further convinced Finley that he was underground with no signal interfering with the Welsh detective and putting the entire operation in danger. He parked his Jaguar at the side of the track as close as he could. The bunker was a few hundred yards from an access road, long since overgrown and abandoned. Its original purpose was to store men and equipment during the Second World War, in case Adolph Hitler invaded Ireland as a stepping-stone to invade the British mainland. Luckily for the Brits, Adolph was too busy being shafted by the Russians to invade the Emerald Isle. More fool him.

After the war, the bunker was locked up and left to rot and during the troubles, the farmer who owned the land offered it to Finley's father as a safe place to store weapons and people on the run from the security services. It was also handy for interrogations, as it was remote and soundproof, and no one had used it for years. Finley had paid the farmer to make sure no one ever used it again, hence they used it as a dumpsite. Once the dust had settled, they would go back and remove the corpse and dispose of it properly. When he turned off the engine and checked the wood, he could see Des Curran's BMW was parked further down the lane. It was a dead end beyond it, nothing but trees for miles.

'I fucking knew it, you dirty perv,' Finley muttered to himself. 'I'm going to cut your bollocks off, so I am.'

He opened the door and climbed out, checking the area before removing a Glock from beneath the passenger seat and a torch from the boot. He slipped it into his jacket and headed along the path towards the entrance. The rusted metal doors were closed but unlocked. The padlock was swinging from the latch in the wind, making a squeaking nose. Des had a key. He must have had one cut because Finley didn't give him one, but that's the type of snake in the grass he was. A man like Des Curran would steal the hole from your donut. Finley grabbed the handle and twisted it. The metal was ice-cold and wet and it protested at being moved with an ear-piercing whine. He pulled the heavy door open, and the stench of damp and mould assaulted his senses. Cold air rushed out to greet him and make him feel unwelcome. The bunker was not a pleasant place to be. He listened for a moment before stepping inside and switching on the torch. The lights worked further down the system of tunnels, but the damp had eroded the wiring near the surface. Closing the doors created a loud bang of metal on metal, which echoed deep down in the bowels of the complex. He headed down the steps which led to the lower levels, knowing Des Curran would have heard him entering the bunker. He'd made enough noise to wake the dead let alone disturb a rapist, but it had been intentional. Whatever the outcome, Des wasn't going to be a happy bunny.

Finley reached the third level, and the lights were burning. The tunnel floor was flooded with water, ankle deep, and he splashed along it in the half light, keeping his torch on to supplement the ancient bulbs, which struggled to illuminate more than a few metres below them, creating dark patches between each one. He stepped up into another corridor, which branched off to the right, and the concrete floor was dry. The room where they'd left the detective was fifty yards further on. No doubt Curran would be pulling up his pants and manufacturing an excuse as to why he'd seen fit to come back to a dump site. No one returns to a dump site unless it's in danger of being compromised. It was a golden rule not to be broken.

As he turned the corner, he saw a body on the floor, the face mangled and swollen around the eyes, the throat slashed. There appeared to be a pen lodged in one of the sockets. It was a terrible sight to behold even when he realised it was Des Curran.

'It looks like you bit off more than you could chew, you silly bastard,' Finley said to himself. 'You got exactly what you deserved and more.'

He couldn't think of anyone who deserved to be slaughtered in such a way, however, the person who had done this to him was nowhere to be seen. Finley stepped over Curran's body and peered into the room where they'd left the detective to die. There was a lot of blood on the floor and some strips of gaffer tape were hanging from the gurney but no sign of her.

The lights went out, and he heard the sound of splashing and then footsteps on the stairs. Reality hit him like a sledgehammer, and he heard the metal doors at the entrance squealing and then the terrifying sound of them slamming closed.

CHAPTER 53

Kim took the padlock from the latch and slid it onto the hasp and staple lock. It was the biggest one she had seen, obviously made to protect a military installation. Her fingers were swollen and painful, but she managed to click the lock home. She turned and ran as fast as she dared along the path through the woods. It was raining and the sound of water dripping from the trees was soothing and she felt free. Being held underground and left to die had rattled her. She needed to be away from that terrible place. The men she had locked in were not there to rescue her, she knew that. She had no idea how many there were. They'd come to finish the job.

As she broke from the trees, she saw a black BMW parked a hundred yards down the path. The keys had a BMW fob attached. She had taken the keys from Des, along with his wallet and phone. Everything which would help to identify him, and the others involved in her kidnap. She knew the ringleader was Veronica Kelly and she would make sure the bitch was dragged back to Wales and locked up for a long time. Life inside wasn't good enough for her, the evil bitch. When she reached the BMW, she was breathless and weak, and her blood loss had sapped her strength. She pressed the unlock button and climbed into the vehicle; it was warm and dry but stank of Des. His stench was engrained in the material and carpets. Sweat and cheap cologne, cigarettes, and alcohol. She inserted the key and turned the ignition and the engine fired up and she put it into first gear and reversed along the path until she had enough room to do a three-point turn. The light was fading, and she switched on the headlights to penetrate the gloom beneath the trees. When she looked up, Patrick Finley was standing on the track, aiming a Glock at her face through the windscreen.

CHAPTER 54

Rio Woods was lying on his bed, staring at his phone. His dad had gone, and his mum was most of the way through a bottle of Aldi whiskey. She had gone through the 'relaxed' phase into the 'overemotional' stage and arrived at the 'everyone's a twat' stage quickly tonight. He still couldn't believe she'd gone on about him wanking in front of his dad. There had been some embarrassing incidents growing up, but that was top of the cringe list. That was so traumatic, he thought about leaving home. Mums across the world must be aware of when their adolescent children become sexually aware and begin exploring and pleasuring themselves, but he was certain none of them said what she had tonight. The wank-stain fairy? Where the fuck did that come from? He would never forget that as long as he lived; that had scarred him deep. No wonder his dad started drinking all day and left home. His mum was a knobhead. As much as he loved her, she was a knobhead. End of story.

Helen replied to his last text. They'd been texting for hours now and the conversation had gone from them being mutually apologetic about what had happened to each other, to full-on flirting. She was shy at first, but she was opening up a bit now. One thing was absolutely clear and that was her genuine regrets about her dad attacking him. She couldn't believe it had happened, and he was milking it, saying she could apologise properly when they meet. She said she would make it up to him. He punched the air when he read that one. Rio reckoned that with right encouragement, he could get a sympathy wank like Cody had when he said his dog died, but he didn't really have a dog. He would have to double check the process with Cody. He was the master of sexual activity and seemed to get it all the time.

Even though his nose was broken, and his nuts were sore and swollen, this was the best result that could have happened. It was going to be worth all the pain and anguish just to full-on snog her. She was such a pretty girl. He read her text, and she was repeating how sorry she was about her dad. She was being so apologetic about what he'd done to him at the school and she couldn't believe he'd gone to the hospital and attacked him again. She was mortified by his actions, and she couldn't believe he'd withdrawn his statement. It had given them a bond and he could feel their attraction growing as they messaged into the night.

Her dad, fucking nutjob Ernie, was banged up in the cells and if what his dad said was right, he was a murderer and would go away for life. With him out of the equation, he would have plenty of time to coax Helen into a relationship without the fear of being smashed into smithereens with a hammer like Wills. That was a different level, but Rio wasn't surprised. He knew how dangerous nutjob Ernie was. When he'd grabbed him in toilets, the look in his eyes was something he didn't want to see again. Rio had no doubt that man could pick up a hammer and use it on another human.

His phone buzzed again, and he read it and replied excitedly. She still wanted him to teach her how to kiss with tongues, but only when her bruising had gone and she didn't look like the Elephant Man. This was getting better and better. She was well up for it. He put his hand down his shorts and touched himself, but then he remembered the wank-stain fairy and it killed the moment.

****

In an evidence bag at Caernarfon's custody suite, Ernest Metcalfe's phone was vibrating each time they sent a message to each other, and each message was in his inbox.

Chapter 55

Kim hesitated and put her foot on the clutch. Whoever had opened the door and gone down into the bunker must have been with this man, or there was another way out of there. The man was tall and rugged looking. He had ex-military written all over him, wide at the shoulders and narrow at the hip. His firing position was textbook. His jaw was set, one eye closed, aiming at the centre of her mass, ready to fire. She had no idea if there were more of them. She looked around and scanned the woods but couldn't see anyone else. In a matter of seconds, the feeling of elation had vaporised. Her freedom had been taken from her and she'd been left for dead with nothing to think about but death itself. It was once more threatened, and she would rather die than be taken back into that hole in the ground. The simple fact was that her life was in grave jeopardy. This man couldn't let her escape because she knew the identity of his employer. If she surrendered, she was dead. If she tried to escape, she was likely to be shot and would probably die, anyway. Fuck it, she thought. She took her foot off the clutch and floored it.

Chapter 56

Olivia was speaking to Paul Campbell, who was head of the RUC Special Branch. He'd been working in counter terrorism for twenty-five years. He was more helpful than anyone else she'd spoken to. She was hoping that his experience and in-depth knowledge of the island and its intricate social balance could help her pinpoint who had Kim. At first, he was wily with his answers, suspicious of her enquiries. Once she explained her dilemma, he relaxed a little.

'I genuinely think this is personal,' Olivia said. 'I can't think of any other reason why they would take her from her home otherwise.'

'I agree with you. It's far simpler to put a bomb under her car or a bullet through her brain,' Paul said. 'Taking a prisoner is a logistical nightmare.' He paused. 'How certain are you that she's here?'

'As certain as we can be,' Olivia said. 'The vans that were used were hired in Liverpool and then boarded the Dublin ferry from Holyhead.'

'And you think she was in the back of one of them?'

'Yes. I do,' she said. 'Nothing else makes sense.'

'You'll not find much sense to things here. The sands are forever shifting and we have our ear to the ground at the moment.'

'Why is that?'

'All communications have either stopped or become encrypted.'

'What does that indicate?' Olivia asked.

'It indicates that there's a shitstorm brewing somewhere, and everyone is battening down the hatches. We know there's going to be something big, but we don't know where or when or what it will be.'

'But do you have any idea why this would be related to the kidnap of a detective inspector from North Wales?' Olivia asked. 'I'm completely baffled.'

'There could be something connecting it. I may have a snifter of information for you, and you will have to investigate it and go digging for the truth,' Paul said. 'A judge from the south has gone missing. His name is Braden Murphy, and he's a decent, honest member of the judiciary. Now, when a judge goes missing, he's either running from a corruption charge, a woman scorned, or something bad has happened to him.'

'Something bad, like what?'

'Like what happened to your detective,' Paul said. 'Taken away in the back of a van and never seen again.'

'And what do you think has happened to him?' Olivia asked.

'It's not our investigation, you know. It's in the south, but when a judge goes missing, you can count on the paramilitaries being involved. If they're bent and taking bribes, they can outlive their usefulness, or the opposite can happen and they won't take a bribe to change the outcome of a case. Sometimes they aren't bent, and they've slapped the wrong man in prison and when I say wrong, I mean he's guilty but dangerous. Some of these people are beyond the law in their own mind and if they get sent down, they seek revenge on anyone involved in getting them sent away.'

'This feels like revenge,' Olivia said. 'I can feel it in my bones.'

'Braden Murphy hasn't used his phone or bank cards since he went missing three days ago, which we both know means he's dead already.'

'What do you think is happening?'

'The catholics are cleaning house, Superintendent. They executed one of their own on your patch, didn't they?'

'Yes. Liam O'Grady,' Olivia said. 'They shot him in the back of the head and tossed him into a reservoir.'

'Did they weigh him down?'

'No. He was floating on the surface.'

'They didn't because they wanted him to be found quickly,' Paul explained. 'They want everyone to know he was an informer and what they do to informers. There will be more before this particular shitstorm blows itself out.'

'What can I do from here?'

'Take a look at any recent deaths that have taken place within the catholic ranks, accidental or otherwise, and look for a connection between our judge and yours. I think Murphy and Preece are connected to something shitty which has happened, and they've unwittingly paid the price.'

'Okay, I'll do that. Thank you,' Olivia said. 'You've been most helpful.'

'My pleasure,' Paul said. 'If you're digging for information over here, keep your head down, Superintendent. The forces here don't take kindly to people snooping into their business and if you rattle the wrong cage, you'll be in danger,' he added. 'You take care of yourself,' he said, hanging up the call.

'You too.'

Olivia ended the call and picked up the desk phone. She felt a glimmer of hope growing in the darkness of not knowing the answers, and it was growing brighter by the minute.

Chapter 57

The BMW's tyres turned, catapulting leaves, mud, and twigs high into the air as it accelerated towards Patrick Finley. Kim ducked down behind the wheel, peering over the dashboard as the engine roared. The power in the vehicle was frightening, and it lurched forward as she accelerated. Finley fired three shots in quick succession and the windscreen exploded into a million pieces, fragments sliced her exposed skin, and she closed her eyes, so as not to be blinded. The wing mirror shattered and disintegrated, and the headrest behind her was torn from its fixings. Kim zigzagged from one side of the track to the other and Finley kept firing. He didn't flinch as the BMW reached halfway between them, accelerating all the time. The bullets whistled and smashed into the vehicle and the dashboard imploded, showering her with shards of speedometer. The on-board media centre was shattered into lethal shards, which whistled past her face and stuck into the seat next to her head. Kim held onto the wheel and felt the crushing impact as the vehicle collided with Finley. His body was launched into the air and she heard him land on the boot before being thrown off into the bushes which lined the track. In the rear-view mirror, she saw him staggering to his feet before falling on his face.

Kim took her foot off the pedal slightly and gained control of the car, but it was still way too fast for her liking. The steering wheel fought against her each time it hit a rock and at every hole in the track. She guided it over the bumps and potholes along the lane as fast as she dared until she reached the main road. Her breathing settled, and she closed her eyes to clear her head and she could feel her blood pumping through her veins. She opened her eyes and checked where she was. It was a T-junction, and the road was empty in both directions. She headed right and hoped it would take her somewhere safe. As she pulled out, she saw headlights piercing the gloom of the forest behind her. There was only one other vehicle on that track, and it was closing the distance between them quickly. Kim cried out in anguish.

'No, no, no, you should be dead, you bastard!'

She put her foot down and freezing cold air poured in through the gap where the windscreen had been. She shivered with the cold as she accelerated, the BMW travelling at over eighty miles per hour as she tried to outrun her pursuer.

Chapter 58

The custody sergeant at Caernarfon was on the phone to Holyhead station; they'd put him on hold. He was against the clock with the man in number eight. Ernest Metcalfe had been charged with a section eighteen assault on his daughter, but there was nothing else of substance to back up any extension of custody. His solicitor was on the other line, threatening court action if he wasn't released immediately. He needed to talk to the detective in charge of the investigation for an update.

'DS Hall,' Chod answered.

'This is Sergeant Morris at Caernarfon. I've got a very pissed off brief on the other line, threatening to sue NWP and you personally, if we don't release his client, Ernest Metcalfe.'

'I know what you're going to say, and we've got nothing but a theory and hot air,' Chod said. 'I've been waiting for an act of God or something similar, but we have nothing to connect him to the murder yet. I know he did it, but we can't prove anything.'

'If you have nothing, I'm going to have to spring him,' the sergeant said, sighing. 'Do you need to keep an eye on him?'

'What do you mean?'

'Is he likely to commit another crime?' the sergeant asked. 'Have you got enough to tag him?'

'Nope. We can't apply a tag or curfew because the assault charge is domestic. His brief will contest it and it will be thrown out,' Chod said, sounding deflated. 'You know how it goes. Let him go for now. I'll have the bastard back in there by the end of the week.'

'That's a confident shout. Put your money where your mouth is,' the sergeant said, laughing. 'Do you want to put a monkey on it?'

'Nope,' Chod said. 'This guy is way too slippery to bet against.'

'Okay. He's out of here.' The sergeant put the phone down and turned to his constables.

'We're springing Metcalfe in number eight,' he said.

'Let me finish my cuppa,' one of the constables said. 'He's not going anywhere. Let him wait until I've finished my KitKat.'

'His brief is blowing a gasket on the other end of this phone,' the sergeant said, pointing to a call on hold. 'That chocolate bar can wait, and I thought you were on a diet, anyway. Go and let him out right now.'

The constables grumbled and made their way down the corridor. The sergeant could hear them moaning and bitching, but it was nothing new. Custody was a cushy shift for some officers, but they still bitched about it. It was the nature of the beast. The cells were quiet for a change. Covid had stifled the amount of heavy drinking taking place in town. Most of the piss-heads stayed at home nowadays where they could only fight with the missus. Assaults were well down, but domestic abuse had gone through the roof.

The officers came back with Ernie, holding his shoes in one hand and his belt and laces in the other.

'Good news, Mr Metcalfe,' the custody sergeant said as he approached the desk. 'You're being released pending further investigations. Here are your belongings,' he added. 'Can you check through them and make sure everything is there, please?'

'Don't make it sound like you're doing me a favour. I shouldn't have been brought here in the first place,' Ernie muttered. He fastened his laces and put on his belt before opening the sealed bag of belongings. His wallet went into his jeans first, and then he picked up his mobile. The Trojan Horse app was flashing. He opened it and felt sick inside. Over a hundred text messages had been sent and received from Helen's phone. His face changed colour and pure rage coursed through his veins. He glanced at some of the latest messages and white heat burnt inside his brain. 'Can you call me a taxi please?' he asked the sergeant. 'I've got something very important to attend to.'

Chapter 59

Kim saw a sign for the R693 and a marker which said it was nine kilometres to Kilkenny. She had never been to Ireland before, but she knew Kilkenny was a reasonably big town and it would have plenty of people and a police station. She glanced at the remains of the dashboard. The BMW was running hot. The temperature gauge was climbing beyond the red and she could smell burning oil as the engine got hotter. She didn't know much about engines, but she knew hot ones are generally fucked and will seize very quickly. A bullet might have pierced the radiator or engine block. Whatever was causing it, she needed it to keep running for nine kilometres. Just nine kilometres. Nine kilometres didn't seem like a long way, but with an overheating engine, it felt like a million miles. The Jaguar was still behind her, and it was gaining. He would be on her if she didn't go faster. She pressed her foot down further at every opportunity she could, but the speed frightened her. The road was fairly straight and there was hardly any traffic, which helped but she was holding the steering wheel so tightly, her knuckles were white. She was beginning to panic when she saw a sign for St Luke's Hospital. She needed a busy place to be able to stop safely, and she needed a doctor. The hospital was the ideal place to head for. Her spirits lifted a little.

The minutes ticked by slowly and the road seemed to stretch on forever. An ambulance went by in the opposite direction, sirens blaring. She wanted to block the road and make them pick her up, but it was too quiet. The man behind her needed her dead and the only thing stopping that from happening was dozens of witnesses. She felt her heartbeat increasing as she approached the entrance. The Jaguar came into view behind her, taking the bend at breakneck speed. The accident and emergency department was directly ahead, and she aimed for it, her vision blurring. She drove into the ambulance bays and hit the kerb with a crunch, ripping the spoiler from the front of the car. She leant forward and pressed her horn. Two uniformed police officers ran towards her car, weapons drawn. They shouted instructions at her, but she was oblivious to them. She leant on the horn with her elbow, while she opened the door with her other hand, almost falling out of the car. Ambulance men approached, seeing her bloody face through the windscreen. She heard them talking to her and asking her what her name was.

'Kim,' she mumbled as they lifted her from the vehicle. From the corner of her eye, she saw the dark Jaguar slowing down as it passed the entrance. It drove on. She felt them putting her onto a trolley and she closed her eyes and slipped into unconsciousness.

Chapter 60

Helen was getting sleepy, but the buzz of attraction was keeping her awake. Adrenalin pumped through her. She didn't want the conversation to end. Rio was so nice and complimentary, and he was so handsome and dreamy. He said she was the prettiest girl in her year, which wasn't true, but it made her blush like never before. That was such a lovely thing to say. He was being so naughty too, teasing her about never being kissed properly. She wanted to kiss him until his face fell off. She'd sent a reply to his last message, but he hadn't replied for ages. Maybe he had fallen asleep, or maybe it was a long message he was typing. She was dropping off to sleep when her phone beeped.

Rio: *My mum's doing my head in. I'm going to kill her.*

Helen: *Why?*

Rio: *Because she's a bitch.*

Helen: *You shouldn't say that. I miss my mum.*

Rio: *She was a bitch too.*

Helen: *Wow. That's nasty.*

Rio: *I am nasty.*

Helen: *What are you talking about?*

Rio: *I'm only being nice to you to get into your knickers.*

Helen: *OMG*

Rio: *Think I'm going to hurt my mum. In fact, I am going to.*

Helen: *If that's your idea of a joke, it's not funny. You shouldn't say stuff like that.*

Rio: *Why not?*

Helen: *Because it's not nice.*

Rio: *I told you I'm not nice. I'm just being nice to you for a reason.*

Helen: *What are you talking about?*

Rio: *You know I'm just being nice because I'm trying to fuck you, don't you?*

Helen: *OMG.*

Rio: *What do you think I'm talking to you for?'*

Helen: *Wow. I thought we were friends.*

Rio: *I'm not your friend. You're just a stupid little girl curious about cocks.*

Helen: *That's so disgusting.*

Rio: *You were all hot for it before?*

Helen: *You asked me about kissing not anything dirty.*

Rio: *One thing leads to another.*

Helen: *Why are you being so horrible?*

Rio: *All the lads in my year have had a bet who can get a smelly finger from you. We've all bet a fiver each. I was just trying to win the bet.*

Helen: *That's sick. I wouldn't let you anywhere near me.*

Rio: *Yes, you would because you're a little slut like your mother.*

Helen: *I'm going.*

Rio: *Me too, for good. Have a nice life.*

Helen: *What changed? OMG. You're a massive weirdo.*

Rio: *See you in hell. Slut.*

Helen wiped tears from her eyes and turned off her phone. She'd heard enough for one night. Her emotions had gone from super-happy to shit in a few minutes. Rio must be bipolar or split personality or something. One minute he was lovely and then he turned into a vile freak. Curious about cocks? OMG. How dare he say that to her? And calling her mum a slut. She wasn't going to speak to that creep ever again.

****

Ernie showered, washing the blood from his hands and face. It turned pale pink as it mixed with the water and circled down the plughole. He didn't like their shower gel. It smelt cheap and soapy. Turning off the water, he wiped down the taps with the towel and then poured a bottle of bleach down the plughole. He put his own clothes into a bin bag and struggled into a tracksuit, which was three sizes too small for him. All the shoes were too small for his feet, so he put his own back on and pulled a pair of socks over them. He put the phone down the toilet but didn't flush it. Gloves and a baseball cap finished his outfit as he gathered his things, stuffed them into a holdall, and headed for the stairs.

Chapter 61

The Next Day

Olivia was discussing the Willis murder with Bill Armstrong, while sorting through the information that had come in overnight. It was early in the morning, but the MIT was already in full swing. The night shift had been busy cross-referencing cases which involved all the victims. Richard Lewis knocked on the door and smiled. His face blushed a little. Olivia gestured for him to come in and sit down. She ended the call.

'Morning, boss,' Richard said.

'Morning,' she said. She noticed he was wearing aftershave, which she hadn't noticed before. She smiled internally. 'Is there anything new on the Willis murder?'

'No. I'm afraid not, but I may have something solid on Kim,' Richard said, straightening a new tie. 'You said to check all paramilitary deaths in Ireland, and I found a suicide at Cork prison, Niall Kelly.'

'Okay, tell me about him,' Olivia said, frowning.

'He was twenty-one when he was sentenced for conspiracy to rob a depository and possession of automatic weapons and ammunition,' Richard said. 'Guess who sent him down?'

'Barden Murphy?' Olivia said, shaking her head.

'Yup,' Richard said. 'The case against him included surveillance from the mainland and cooperation from NWP. And guess which two detectives gave evidence via an internet link?'

'Please tell me it was Alan and Kim.'

'Okay. It was Alan and Kim,' Richard said, nodding. 'And the judge who granted all the surveillance requests was…'

'Belinda Preece,' Olivia said, picking up the phone. 'So, it was revenge. It has to be his family, yes?'

'Definitely.'

'What do we know about them?'

'His father vanished when he was a child, but his mother, Veronica Kelly, is thought to be involved with paramilitary groups in the south and a detective in Dublin told me she's well up the ranks, a senior advisor,' Richard explained. 'When I told him about Kim, he said Veronica is an evil bitch and if she has Kim, don't expect to get her back in one piece.'

'That is excellent work, Richard,' Olivia said. 'I need to get Diane Warburton involved. We need the big guns to have Veronica Kelly arrested and interviewed. I just hope it's not too late for Kim.'

CHAPTER 62

Patrick Finley hung up the call and climbed out of the Jaguar. Veronica was furious, but she only had herself to blame. Revenge had blinded her and made her incapable of making a rational decision. It was an impossible operation to pull off without attracting the attention of law enforcement on the mainland. Shooting British police officers was never a good idea because they had unlimited resources and long memories. He had warned her until he was blue in the face, but she came up with a plan to kidnap the Davies woman and put the blame on a local petty criminal on Anglesey. It was destined for failure. The police may have followed the trail she laid at first, but they're not stupid. Veronica had broken so many golden rules during her half-cocked revenge spree that he'd lost count of them. The focus of her attention now was the women who could categorically identify her as her kidnapper. DI Kim Davies was in surgery and would be under anaesthetic for a while, but not for long and when she woke up and came around, she'd be singing like a canary. Veronica told him to make sure she didn't.

CHAPTER 63

Jimmy Woods knocked on the door for the third time. He had a carton of milk, a loaf of bread, and a packet of smoked bacon in his shopping bag. Rio loved bacon butties and a mug of tea in the morning, but his mum rarely had any in. She spent all her money on whiskey and cigarettes. Jimmy felt guilty for not being able to protect his son from Metcalfe. He felt guilty for leaving him with his mother when he left, but the boy was better off with her. Kids are usually better off with their mothers in his opinion. Jimmy was under no illusions about his capacity to bring up a teenage boy when he lived in a one-bedroom flat and spent all his social money on ale. He had borrowed a tenner to buy the breakfast, but it was a gesture to show his son that he loved him. A glance at his watch told him he had been there for fifteen minutes. Wendy still hadn't opened the door, and he was cold. He knocked again, not wanting to look through the letter box. Wendy had a knack of throwing stuff in his face when he looked in. She would stand next to the door hiding behind the wall, waiting for him to lift the flap just to throw tea in his face. She threw piss at him once, but that was when she found out he was screwing the barmaid from the Blossoms. It wasn't his finest moment, but she must have planned it in her head. No one just has a cup of piss handy to chuck in the face of their cheating husband. What type of wife does that?

'Wendy!' he shouted and knocked again. No reply. He picked up a pebble from the garden and threw it at Rio's bedroom window. Still nothing. There was nothing left but to look through the letter box. He lifted the flap and peered inside. What he saw took his breath away, and he staggered backwards and fell off the step, landing in a heap on the grass.

Chapter 64

Chod and Richard waited for the locksmith to open the door. A cordon had been made to keep concerned neighbours and Jimmy Woods back from the house. Jimmy was screaming Rio's name at the top of his voice. Some neighbours were trying to calm him down, but he was inconsolable. The detectives were wearing scene suits when they entered. Uniformed officers were busy checking the gardens, front and back.

'Jesus,' Richard said, shaking his head. 'She's been stabbed multiple times.' A large kitchen knife protruded from her chest. 'We need to arrest the ex-husband and get him away from here.'

'The doors and windows are all locked,' Chod said. 'Let's take a look upstairs.'

Chod went first and reached the landing where the smell of death met him. He glanced in the bathroom, which was small and consisted of a shower cubicle, sink, and toilet. He spotted the mobile down the toilet.

'We need to bag that,' he said to Richard.

Richard nodded and picked it out of the water. He dropped it into an evidence bag, and they moved to the bedrooms. The master contained a double bed, wardrobe, and chest of drawers. All the furniture was tired and dated. The single bedroom door was closed. Chod turned the handle and pushed it open slowly. Rio was hanging from the wardrobe door, a belt around his neck, eyes bulging from his face, tongue protruding from his mouth. A footstool was toppled on the floor beneath him.

'He's stabbed his mother and then topped himself?' Richard said. Chod nodded.

'It looks like that, doesn't it?' Chod said.

'Do still want the ex-husband arrested?' Richard asked.

'I don't think that's necessary anymore,' Chod said. 'The poor bastard will be distraught enough as it is. He's no longer a suspect.'

CHAPTER 65

Ernie filled the holdall full of rocks and tossed it from the headland into the sea. Wendy Woods' blood, skin, and hair would be all over the clothes he'd been wearing when he stabbed her; as were traces from Rio. It was such a waste, but the stupid little pervert hadn't listened to the warnings he gave him. He didn't listen and worse than that, he persisted in trying to groom Helen into a sexual relationship. A thirteen-year-old child. Some people can't be persuaded or coerced with polite requests to desist in their behaviour. He'd spoken to him in a peaceful manner, but the common-sense approach had been ignored. Sometimes violence is the only answer, but society doesn't tolerate that so, he had to employ a skill set from his younger life. There were no emotions, no regrets, no sympathy. Rio Woods had been given several chances to stay away from his daughter and he chose to ignore them all. Ernie had to protect her, and he would continue to protect her and her sisters until they were old enough to protect themselves.

The texts he sent to Helen on Rio's phone would make her think twice the next time an older boy from school came sniffing around. She would wonder if it was part of a bet. They would also give the police an insight into what happened. Rio had told her he wanted to hurt his mother and by the looks of it, he had. Murder suicides are more common these days. Ernie had no alibi as the girls were at his mother's, but he'd waved at them through the window when he got back from Caernarfon and left his lights on and his phone in the bedroom. He'd walked to town across the golf course and there was no evidence at the scene to suggest he was involved. On the face of it, the Woods were a tragic example of how teenagers' mental health issues had spiralled downwards through covid. Teenage suicides were up. Rio Woods had cried like a baby and begged for his life, but he had no one to blame but himself. There could be no mercy for any man approaching his daughters even if she encouraged him. Simple. Slut.

CHAPTER 66

Patrick Finley used the back entrance of the hospital and walked through the orthopedic department to reach the lifts. Kim Davies was in the ICU recovering from surgery. Veronica Kelly was on her way to Dublin Police Station with her solicitor. Detectives had attended her home and told her she was to be interviewed about the kidnap of a British detective and that she could attend voluntarily, or she would be arrested. Her situation was dire. The disappearance of Barden Murphy had a similar effect as poking a bear with a sharp stick. Law enforcement agencies were ramping up the pressure in response. Something had to give.

Finley took the lift to the third floor and put on his balaclava. Kim would be in the ward directly opposite, and the doors were unlocked. They were usually locked, but one of the porters was an ally. The doors opened and Finlay took a step out of the lift, removing his Glock. Three special branch officers aimed their weapons at him.

'Drop the weapon, Patrick,' one of them ordered. 'We know what you're doing, and we know who you're doing it for but there's no need for you to die here today.'

'You know what happens if I fail,' Patrick said, shaking his head. He paused for a millisecond, but raised his weapon an inch. The officers opened fire and Finlay crumpled beneath a hail of nine-millimetre bullets.

CHAPTER 67

Twelve Months Later

Ernie picked the girls up from school and they headed into Holyhead to Tesco to buy some supplies for their lunchboxes. The girls chattered about school gossip and what was going on with their friends. Helen had settled down and almost forgiven him, but not quite. Ernie had tried hard to express how sorry he was that he'd hit her. He begged her forgiveness over and over and she yielded although they still had visits from a social worker. He was her father, after all, and she understood he was just trying to protect her. She still didn't know how he'd found out about Rio messaging her in the first place, and they didn't talk about it. It was best left in the past. Ernie kept an eye on all of their communications, and he always would, just to be sure they were safe and no one was taking advantage. Even when they became adults, he would need to check their safety. Boyfriends and husbands could be abusive and manipulating. They could be cheats and liars, and he would make sure his girls were treated with respect. That was his job.

They parked up and went inside. Helen grabbed a trolley and they headed for the chilled aisle so they could stock up on sandwich fillings, milkshakes, and yogurts. Ernie was reaching for a six-pint carton of semi-skimmed when he felt the first blow. The knife penetrated him beneath his outstretched arm, cracking his ribs before piercing his lung. His knees buckled, and he knelt. The second blow pierced his neck where it meets the collarbone, driving down into the aorta. Arterial spray covered his daughters, splattering their faces with his blood. Jimmy Woods carried on stabbing him long after Ernie was dead.

CHAPTER 68

Alan and Kim were sitting in Caernarfon Crown Court, waiting to give evidence via an internet connection in the case against Veronica Kelly, who had been on remand for over a year. Two of her cronies had turned evidence against her and she was looking at life for the kidnap and murder of Judge Barden Murphy. The Irish authorities were in no rush to allow the Brits to get their hands on her. The kidnap and imprisonment of Kim was inconsequential to their case, but they were keen to hear their evidence. It was the best they could do.

'Any joy yet?' Olivia Mann walked in with a tray of tea and coffee.

'Thanks, Olivia,' Alan said. 'Kim is usually the tea lady.'

'I've been demoted,' Kim said, smiling. 'I lost the title when I was kidnapped, but if you snooze, you lose.'

'You can have the job back when you're ready,' Olivia said. 'I'm just keeping it warm for you.'

'Nah. Keep it,' Kim said. 'It's about time he did it himself, anyway.'

'I've got a bad knee,' Alan said.

'You've got a bad everything,' Kim said. 'I doubt he knows where the kettle is.'

'What kettle?'

Kim touched the pink scar on her neck. It tingled sometimes and still felt numb in places. The surgeons said it was normal and the feeling may never return to how it was before. She could live with that, although her nightmares were still with her. She would awake clawing at a mask on her face, desperately trying to breathe. It was diagnosed as post-traumatic stress disorder and they offered her pills, which she declined. There wasn't a pill on the planet which would dull the memories of her incarceration, the visit from Des Curran, fighting for her life and being stabbed, and finally slitting his throat. She would sweat and panic when she thought of it. The Garda had questioned her about Curran's death, exploring the level of violence she employed to escape him. She had even questioned herself. Maybe she could have escaped and let him live. Fuck him.

Alan stood up and walked to the window, a visible limp in his gait. The turrets of Caernarfon Castle towered above the town. He remembered a jolly boys' outing to the castle with his friends from his local at the Driftwood in Trearddur Bay. It was a pub crawl by any other name.

'Did you see the poppies from the Tower of London when they brought them to the castle?' he asked.

'No. I missed that,' Kim said.

'They made a giant dragon's claw out of them,' Alan said. He showed her a photograph on his phone. It showed his friends standing together inside the walls. 'They all look quite sober there.'

'I'm sure that didn't last long,' Kim said. 'You should arrange another one as soon as you can. Life is too short,' she added.

Printed in Great Britain
by Amazon